THE **87**
RULES
FOR
COLLEGE

THE 87 RULES FOR COLLEGE

Jake Shore and Drew Moffitt

New Chapter Press

ISBN: 978-1937559571

Published by New Chapter Press
1175 York Ave, Suite #3s
New York, NY 10065
Randy Walker, Managing Partner
RWalker@NewChapterMedia.com
www.NewChapterMedia.com

The 87 Rules For College is distributed by the Independent
Publishers Group (www.IPGBook.com)

Disclaimer: All names and identifying details in this book
are fiction.

WARNING

The following does not advocate, encourage or
promote debauchery.
All characters and events are fictional.

INTRODUCTION

College is like a great meal a pricey restaurant: you're hungry for it, there's lots of anticipation, you gotta make sure you didn't forget your wallet at the beach or wherever the hell it is you just were, but if the food is prepared well, the restaurant is pleasant, and truly good people are at the table eating with you, it's gonna be an awesome, wholesome, memorable, tasty goddamn experience.

RULE # -2
THIS IS NOT A "HOW TO" BOOK

Is this book telling you to actually act out everything that occurs in it? No. Not at all. A lot of what's in here is to show you what not to do, and how to avoid common things that gets kids thrown out, flunked out and displeased about college. This book is *advice*.

RULE # -1
THIS BOOK IS THE ADVICE YOU NEED TO AVOID THE ROOKIE MISTAKES

RULE # -1(A)
DON'T MAKE ROOKIE MISTAKES

RULE # -1(B)
ROOKIE MISTAKES GET YOU KICKED OUT OF COLLEGE

RULE # -1(C)
ROOKIE MISTAKES CREATE BAD TIMES

You gotta get into college and be fifty steps ahead. You gotta be ready. You only do this dance once, and if you don't know the moves, how the dance goes down and the ways to make it the best it can be, you're selling yourself short.

RULE # 0
READ RULE #1

You're not gonna wanna get into college without reading the first rule...

RULE #1

DON'T TRY TOO HARD TO BE THE SHIT

When you arrive to college, it often feels like there's pressure to reinvent yourself. You want to leave the young, naive, unaware, high-school version of yourself behind, right? Sort of.

Yes, you're in college, but the last thing you want to do is to try to be something you're not. A genuine person has more stock than a sleazy, worthless junk bond. It's the pathological liar with a chip on his shoulder the size of a two ton boulder trying way too hard to be the best and know everything who will be revealed as a phony before classes start. It's real easy to spot someone who's trying every cheap trick in the book to assert dominance. There's nothing wrong with trying to be funny and charming, but if you're way outside your personality comfort zone, it's going to be obvious to everyone.

No one likes a liar. Liars lie, and there's no point lying about how many beers you can drink, the tremendous amount of sexual escapades you've had, or that time you went to Vegas, met Scarlett Johansson, convinced her you were Mark Zuckerberg's long lost cousin who truly invented Facebook, and even though Mark took all the credit, he gave you half the money, so Scarlett married you right there in Vegas, but after being hitched for a few hours and loving Scarlett in ways hordes of women and men would sacrifice essential parts of their own anatomy to experience, you decided you and Scarlett weren't compatible and needed some space, because it's right around this point people are going to recognize you're lying and see you're full of shit and deem you not worth a second of their goddamn time. This includes the person or people you want to date, to the potential lifelong friends you'll make in the very first days of college.

Bottom line, just be yourself. People are most drawn to those who are truthful about who they are. Calmness is attractive, and if everyone's running around like a goddamn jackass while you're cool, relaxed and collected, it's going to reflect well.

RULE #2

DON'T PLAGIARIZE

One of the absolute dumbest moves you can make is to plagiarize in college. Whether you like it or not, this is an issue that every institution of higher education takes seriously. There are entire sections and divisions of whatever college you're attending devoted to catching kids who plagiarize and bringing them to justice. It may sound crazy, you may not agree with it, but it doesn't fucking matter. It's just the way it is. It doesn't make a difference if you're writing an English paper, a Psychology one, or taking an Astronomy take-home quiz that you thought you could study for by lying on your back on a patch of grass in front of the main cafeteria last night while staring up at the stars and eating a brownie Leonard Mishim bought at a marijuana dispensary in Colorado. In the midst of that pot-induced haze, gazing up at the beautiful cosmos, you may have believed that you were learning every mystery of the universe, and each answer on the Astronomy take-home test was somehow being documented in your mind. But sadly, when you settle down to take that Astronomy take-home test, the answers haven't magically appeared in your subconscious because you went stargazing on a pot brownie.

If you're at all worried that you don't know exactly what plagiarism is or how to avoid it, it's

THE 87 RULES FOR COLLEGE

a bright idea to consult your student handbook, review the syllabus, or ask your professor for clarification. Below is a list of a few stupid things that are pretty common forms of plagiarism and other things that aren't that stupid that will help you with this issue.

1. Google stuff
   a. This isn't rocket science, people. If you have to write a paper on Ernest Hemingway's The Old Man and the Sea, about that old dude who catches a fish, and you Google something like 'Old Man in the sea papers, please, so I don't have to write one,' and an essay pops up that's been written by someone else that isn't you, and you then print off that paper that you didn't write and hand it into your professor with your name at the top even though you didn't write the goddamn paper, it's a truly remarkable example of plagiarism. Depending on what school you're at, you could definitely get thrown out permanently for doing this. No questions asked. If you get caught plagiarizing this badly the school will kick you the fuck out so fast you won't remember what flavor of fish they're serving at your favorite stir fry station in the central dining

hall. They'll leave you on the goddamn sidewalk crying. Most colleges not only won't care, they won't even blink as they send your sorry ass packing out of the dorms with your college sweatshirt in hand and student loan debt coming out of your ass. You think your college really cares all that much about you? College is a business like any other, and there are plenty more of you where you came from who are ready and willing to take your place. #CollegeTruthHurts.

2. Formatting stuff
    1. In some cases, if you don't format something correctly, it's considered plagiarism. For example, if you're writing a paper on the universe, and you find a legitimate outside source that clarifies how time travel works and what needs to happen in order for humans to enter the fifth dimension without causing an absolutely massive rift in the space time continuum, and you want to use a direct quote from that source in your own paper, you have to make sure you cite the direct quote correctly or you can be accused of plagiarism. In theory, if you format a direct quote incorrectly, you're using someone else's words as your own. Bottom line is,

be careful and be aware of all this shit. Follow whatever formatting guidelines are given, and if you have any questions at all about anything ask your professor about it. If your professor is a dick, then either ask the head of whatever department your class is apart of, or ask your advisor. Once you've been accepted to a school, enrolled, and you're forking over tons of cash every semester, you have the right to get the answers you want, and if that means sending a goddamn letter to the president of the college, then fucking do it.

RULE #3

BLACKING OUT IS BAD

Everyone has nights that get away from them, but nothing good comes from a blackout.

There's nothing wrong with having a few drinks, but if you're so drunk you try to flush yourself down the toilet, you gotta get a grip.

RULE #4

SEARCH AND FEED

There are going to be, and probably already are, plenty of people telling you what to do, what to need, and what to want out of your college experience; however, college at its core is a time for you to explore what it is you'll one day do in the world, and who you want to be. It's a time to search for yourself, and feed the things within you that are in need.

For example: Janice Ryan, a kind girl with strong values and morally sound desires, wanted badly to make the exploration of science her absolute top priority in every way during her college experience. She entered into a medium-sized college and embarked on a major in Biology. She was the type of person who thrived off a typical classroom environment, and once on campus she found engaging and passionate professors who fostered her needs. It was a wonderful direction for her to take. Class inspired and excited her, and even distracted her from the fact that her roommate was fit for a straight jacket.

Nevertheless, Janice enjoyed taking time off from her studies of evolution and taxonomy to attend the occasional party and have a beer or two with her fellow classmates. She found the company of those who enjoyed reading and writing the most pleasant, but even still, she did have an affinity for strange and outlandish men that drank too much beer and skipped class often. She didn't falter, though, and while there were forces during her time in the second semester freshman year that tempted assignment neglect and disengagement from her studies, every time such an urge surfaced, she'd remember how much she was paying for her schooling, and it'd lead to the conclusion that she needed to keep studying.

At the tail end of her freshman year, Janice went to see a stand-up comedian who was performing on campus. She couldn't believe how funny the stand-up was. Some of the jokes awakened feelings she hadn't felt since the moment of her birth, and once she realized that the stand-up comedian had actually made her recall the second she was born, it remained seared in her mind that she may want to try performing jokes.

Soon her studies took a backseat to joke writing, which dominated an incredible amount of her time. Janice could not stop writing jokes, and even though she tried again and again to stop writing the observational humor that forced her to chuckle and laugh and even forget about all the unpleasant things that happen in the world, she found she couldn't stop writing jokes, not one bit, and she also couldn't study. The need to be a joke-maker consumed Janice so thoroughly that she even began wearing oversized shoes and strange makeup designed to make her look more like Ronald MacDonald than a college student. The flower that she wore on her jacket spat out water when someone put their nose too close, and she even put ghost chili pepper flakes in the water so that if someone did get too close to the flower, Janice shot some of the water in his eye and it burned like hell because of the ghost chili flakes. Not only did Janice howl in laughter at the sight of this idiot with ghost chili flakes in his eyes, but others passing by also laughed at him, until someone came over and asked if he was alright and whether or not he needed medical attention.

As another gag, Janice installed a fart machine in the back of a centrally located classroom. The fart machine made a farting noise every nine seconds. The noises varied in intensity and volume, and they were so funny, Tim Rightwood, a junior soccer player, laughed with such force that he needed a double hernia operation. Also, the fart machine was so small and undetectable Professor Blunkus didn't know the machine existed and attributed the noises to the change in food services that had occurred only months before. He began having delusions that the odorless farts coming from the fart machine were either due to the ground beef that was put in the tacos that day, or some type of spoiled seared beef that'd been inexplicably put in the eggs that morning. Eventually, the fart machine confused and angered Professor Blunkus so much that he questioned whether there was any kind of high moral constant in the universe, and began lecturing exclusively about how to prepare a ham and cheese sandwich, instead of accounting.

Skipping class to write jokes turned into skipping class to stand out in the center of campus and repeat jokes over and over again on a loop at the top of her lungs, and Janice had no idea how to get a hold of herself, her education, or what was going to happen with the rest of her college experience.

Ultimately, in the middle of her sophomore year, Janice did regain some sense of her studies, switched her major to English, graduated with a degree, and now writes for a humor magazine in Biloxi, Mississippi.

RULE #5

'NO' DOES NOT MEAN 'YES'

It's clear if someone doesn't want to hook up with you. If you're kissing and things escalade in a natural and positive way, then all is going smooth, but there's a gigantic difference between A) hooking up with someone properly and B) advancing after she (or he) has clearly stated she (or he) isn't into it.

If someone says 'no' when you're trying to hook up, it means no. It's that simple. A willing participant needs no convincing.

RULE #6

THROW THE BEST PARTIES

Most life-changing parties don't fall out of the sky. They're not attached to meteorites piercing through the earth's atmosphere and landing on your doorstep like a sign from aliens to party correctly. In order to have a truly great party you gotta put some effort in. You think Jay-Z plans his own bashes? No. He hires the best party planner on the planet to ensure his birthdays are off the chain. So unless you've got Taylor Swift texting you asking if she can come through your spot with Victoria's Secret and Gucci models, start thinking of ways to get fine looking buts at your party and ensure they'll have a bitchin' enough time to stick around.

A new party is like a new goddamn person. You don't know what she's like. Sure, she might look fantastic and seem cool, but after a few minutes of hanging with her you may find she's a complete asshole. If you're gonna plan a party people will show up for and stay as long as humanely possible out of fear another party this raging might never exist, you've got to get your shit together.

Invites matter. It doesn't matter if you use Facebook, Instagram, Twitter, Tinder, some type of social media that hasn't even been invented yet, or the fucking actual, slug-along, not-moving, why-the-fuck-does-it-still-exist mail, it's not all that important how it's getting there, but you gotta make the invitations to your party awesome. It's gotta be memorable. If it doesn't stand out, it's shit.

When you get an invite to something on Facebook, how judgmental are you? If you're the type who gladly goes to everything you're invited to, then that's great for you, but if you're judgmental and you're constantly looking for reasons to ridicule everything, pointing out why it's all lame, aim those powers of perception at the invitations you're gonna make for this party, and make them great.

Where is it? What band's playing? Is there valet parking? What games will there be? What beer is sponsoring it? What vodka is sponsoring it? What rum is sponsoring it? Is there a wall you can write on? Is there gambling?

If your answer is *no* to any of the questions outlined above you need to get it together.

What beer is sponsoring it? Any goddamn beer you want is sponsoring it. If you put on a Facebook invitation that Schlitz is sponsoring your fucking party and people show up and there's Schlitz everywhere and people are shot-gunning Schlitz, then people will think Schlitz sponsored your party. I don't care if you're in a shitty dorm room or the nicest house on campus.

"Did Schlitz really sponsor this party?"

"They sure fucking did! Cheers! Grab another one!"

If you act like everything's cool and going smooth, people will think it is until you prove them wrong.

"Did Schlitz really sponsor this party?"

"Nope, but it's hilarious, right? Cheers! Grab another one!"

Saying a beer sponsored a party you're throwing when you really just went to the deli and bought a bunch of beer is priceless.

Where's the valet parking? If you put on your party's invitation that there's gonna be valet parking and you live in a fucking dorm room it's great. Maybe even dress one of your friends up as the valet guy?

"Where's the valet parking?"

"Right there! Look, he's wearing a fucking suit! Cheers! Grab another beer!"

Tell your buddy to wear a suit and be the valet guy, or you can be the valet guy, and if you're a girl, get one of your guy friends to dress up in a suit and be the valet guy. Or break all the gender rules and have a valet girl! Things are getting totally fucking insane!

People want to go to parties that are incredibly memorable. They want to see and hear things that they'll remember for the rest of their lives.

Give them that party.

Get one of your buddies to jump over a keg into a small pool filled with whipped cream or something. Put that right on the fucking invitation and see how many people show. Make it a smoking hot chick and it'll be a story you tell for the rest of your fuckin' life.

What band is playing? Live music's the shit. Whether you're throwing a rager in a tiny-ass dorm room, a decent sized suite, or a giant fucking house, the place's size doesn't matter, there's always a way and good reason to get some live music going. It sets a party apart.

Let's say you're living in a dorm room. Not the most ideal living situation in the world, but you've gotta work with what you've got, right? There's no time for bitching and moaning, groaning and complaining about where you're living, people. You've gotta make the most of whatever the college Gods bless you with.

The college Gods are good and fine, generous and wise; they're the ones who came up with the whole idea for college in the first place. I mean, who really thinks this is any way to become an adult? Seriously. Think about it. Put a bunch of 18-21 year-olds in a glorified small village with no real police presence or need to do such human things as cook, clean, make money, drive or work hours that make any fucking sense at all. At best, most classes meet for three hours a week total. Three fucking hours a week? How is it possible that high school, a time when children wake at 7:00 am to get to school by 8:00 am for a full work day, five days a week, is the step BEFORE entering into a higher educational arena where having fun is the absolute highest objective in lieu of things like: normal work hours, a realistic sleep cycle, preparing your own nourishment, not sledding on cafeteria trays, or interacting with adults?

Seriously, aside from the Professors, college is an adult-free zone. It's like never-never land, for fuck's sake.

[Note: When it snows, "borrowing" cafeteria trays to use as sleds is a great way to sled. The snow doesn't have to suck. Yeah, it's cold, but when you're beaming down a hill on campus on a sled you just ate chicken wings off of, you're gonna feel alive as hell.]

In any event, the point is, you can spend your entire college experience bitching and whining about where you live and why it isn't as cool as the president's pad, or a house some sorority has been living in for the last two hundred years, or the dorm at the top of the hill with the Jacuzzi, or the place down near the lake with a bar on the second floor and a Shake Shack attached, but college is short and sweet so stop your belly-aching and start having the time of your life.

There are going to be plenty of these types of nay-saying assholes all throughout your college career. They will be the ones complaining constantly about how much better some other living situation is than their own, and maybe even your own, and why "this sucks" and "this place sucks" and "some other place is way fucking better." Their energy can only be a detriment to you. Yes, it's fine to desire a better place to live, but if there's no way out of the shack, hut, tent, shanty or dorm you're living in for a the foreseeable future, suck it up and make the best out of it.

So, anyway. Live music.

Singer-songwriters are always a pretty good bet. There's definitely no shortage of them, and if you're having a party in a dorm room or a suite, it's probably your best bet considering the amount of space you're working with. A cute chick who plays guitar and sings? Are you kidding me? People eat that shit with a fork and bendy straw.

If you've got a house or decent-sized suite, definitely get a band. You can probably squish a full band into a dorm room if you really want to. Get their drummer to bring out the bongos or some shit and save space and get the tunes going. There's an energy and vibe created by live music, and it gets people excited, dancing and ready to rage.

Don't know a band? Ask around. Somebody is bound to know someone who plays, and as far as payment goes, just tell the band they can drink for free. They're gonna be so happy to actually have a gig it probably isn't even gonna take the free drinks to convince them.

What games will there be? Ideally, you want to offer as many games as possible. There's only so much time people want to spend standing around and getting drunk. Beer pong is a good bet, but games like quarters, kings, asshole, chandeliers and others are good to have going, too.

What's chandeliers?

- Similar in nature to quarters, chandeliers is played on a table and the object is to bounce a quarter off the table into a cup of beer. What distinguishes chandeliers from quarters is, instead of having one cup of beer set down in the middle of the table, each player has their own cup of beer that's placed on the table. The quarter gets passed around, and the object is to bank the quarter into one of your opponents drinking cups. If you bounce the quarter into Johnny's drink, then Johnny drinks. If you bank it into Maria's drink, she drinks. If you fuck it up and bank it into your own drink, then you drink.

Excite someone with kick-ass music, games and hilarious shenanigans and it'll get them ready to party their ass off. Now, you gotta make sure there are plenty of women, which is party planning 101, and a carefully thought out, well executed plan is the first step to having more women around than air molecules. If you're a girl, this is probably pretty easy. You invite all your girlfriends; bada bing, bada boom. For a guy, it's more of a challenge. People want to think, know and thoroughly believe they're gonna go the best party of all time. Any good party needs women, and the best party of all time has so many women you're looking around and thinking, "Wow, there are a lot of women here. This is fucking good.

Really good. If there were more women it might be even better, but for now, considering there are quite a few women here, and that one with the big jugs just looked at me, this is a pretty fucking awesome party." It doesn't really matter what sex you are, either, because everyone will be thinking this shit. Women like to see other women around. If a woman sees there are a shitload of women at a party, they're happy they aren't the only ones.

RULE #6(A)

PEOPLE LIKE THEME PARTIES

Themes are the shit. People love 'em. It's one of the fundamental party elements that separates you from the schmuck who just buys a 30 pack and sits on his couch. Yeah, that might work once or twice to get things going. It isn't unreasonable to believe a 30 pack and a dream can start the greatest party ever thrown, but if you really wanna stick it to the college Gods and let 'em know who's boss over and over again on a consistent basis, assign a theme to your fuckin' party.

<u>THEMES</u>

Lingerie: Lingerie parties are known for getting way the fuck out of hand. We're talking the cops show up and a bunch of people go to jail. A masterfully planned and executed lingerie party has the potential to turn into an all-out naked party, and if you're wondering what a naked party is, you're a fuckin' idiot. Naked parties are like the aurora borealis, except it's a few steps away from an orgy. If you're able to orchestrate a great lingerie party, you're basically a goddamn hero. It isn't easy. It's possibly the most difficult theme party to throw, and it's one of the many reason why we've listed it first. Set your sights high, right?

Why is it so hard? You have to convince a ton of women that it isn't weird to show up to a party in their underwear. I don't care what sex you are, this isn't an easy task. This theme is nothing to scoff at. It's like seeing a piece of sweet and sour chicken that's six thousand degrees and thinking, "Fuck it, I can handle it," and just swallowing the thing whole. You gotta think this through.

One way to approach this is to disguise it as a beach party.

Beach: It's been done thousands of times before and will occur again and again right into infinity. By switching the focus and labeling your bash a "beach" party instead of a "lingerie" party there are pros and cons, and many factors to take into account. Yes, bathing suits are basically the same thing as your underwear, but people don't think twice about this reality once they sit their ass on the beach. In normal society, if a chick's skirt is too short she's considering a slut and menace, but if she's on the beach people are thinking, "Why the fuck is that chick wearing a skirt? Why isn't she just wearing a thong?"

There's nothing wrong with throwing a beach party. Get sand from wall to wall for anyone cares, do whatever the fuck you want, but just realize when your party's theme is beach and not lingerie, there are some differences you're gonna have to come to grips with. It's the truth. Lingerie is a completely different ball of wax, but really, if you wanna have a banging ass beach party, go right ahead. It's really a good option.

It's not good to be so hard on the beach party. It's a fine opportunity to have all kinds of Caribbean-themed drinks. Go with rum, tequila, punch, margaritas, coronas, straw hats, straw skirts, lays, hula hoops, little pools you fill up with water and swim around in, and everything else under the sun you can think of. Go nuts, you're at the beach. What do you do at the beach that's fun? Volleyball? Frisbee? Have all that shit right in your house or you dorm room. Also, don't feel discouraged if all you've got is a dorm room. Slam as much shit into that space as you possibly can. Use it all. Every nook and cranny. And don't worry if you don't have any money. None of that matters. Go to the dollar store and get supplies and decorations and get the cheapest booze on the planet. You've got to make some memories here, people, by any means necessary. There's no time to bitch and moan about how little room you got; there are great parties to be had. It's also fun to have a beach party in the winter. People are cold and hating it and then you come along telling them about a ripper where they get to feel like they're at the fucking beach and now you got asses in the seats.

But back to the lingerie party.

Lingerie, continued: There are a few key ingredients for setting up a successful lingerie party.

1) **Get the wonderful woman to help plan the party.**
   a) Who is this wonderful woman? That's up to you. If you are a woman, then you are the wonderful woman. Congratulations. But if you're a guy, you need the wonderful woman. If there's one girl who's into the party, it immediately ups your chances that this party's gonna happen by about, roughly, if the calculations are correct, 58 million billion times. This wonderful woman is the key to majesty, and in order for the entire thing to go down you need to choose this wonderful woman (or women) wisely. You have to approach this woman with a well thought out plan, not a whim that you concocted while hammered and ordering take out Chinese. Your ability to drunkenly order the number 7 combination platter at the local Chinese food place and get it delivered does not mean you're

able to successfully throw a lingerie party. The two aren't mutually exclusive. You gotta have a plan. When you present the idea of a lingerie party to the wonderful woman, the person that will become your partner in making this lingerie party happen, you have to convince her thoroughly that it's going to be one of the best parties of the semester, and she's gonna want to help to make it happen. This is no easy task. As we said, if you're a girl and you're trying to plan one of these parties, you're already in pretty great shape. Just make sure that you and some of your girlfriends are at the party in tasteful lingerie and you've got a lingerie party. Other girls will arrive and realize it's legit and then guys will show up and you're an hour away from some crazy shit to start happening. But if you're a guy and you're trying to plan this, you need to pool all of your collective resources to find either this one wonderful woman who wants to help you plan it, or even an entire group of women. A sorority perhaps? Maybe you know that one kinda crazy chick in a sorority? Or two? How about three? Or maybe there's a wild, awesome chick two floors down or down the street or who cares where the fuck she lives? You gotta convince the wonderful woman. How do you that? You gotta have a plan.

b) Get a bartender

   i) Make someone the bartender. Don't have a bar? Fucking make one. You can think of something, MacGyver. It doesn't have to be anything official or even legitimate, it just has to pass for a bar. Put a sheet on your desk or some shit It doesn't matter. Just get it done. You want a bartender at your party. Treat every party like it's your last. You gotta make it memorable. "Hey, you're all looking really great tonight. Feel free to ask the bartender for whatever you'd like. There's a whole list of mixed drinks."

   (1) **Make a drink menu for the bar.** These don't even have to be the most complicated drinks in the world, but people love the experience of going up to a bar and ordering a drink. Make up the drink names if you want. Below are some examples.

   (a) The Drunken Sailor: Vodka and orange juice.

   (b) The Tipsy Housewife: Vodka and orange juice.

   (c) The Headless Horseman: Vodka and orange juice.

   (d) The Rusty Trombone: Rum and pineapple juice.

   (e) The Continental: Tequila and pineapple juice.

    (f) You get the idea. Just make up a funny name and a simple drink. If you wanna get more complicated with your drink selection, then go for it. Add vermouth or lemonade or whatever other shit you want to make the drinks taste better.

c) **Multiple games:** People don't want to be just sitting around in their underwear.
- i) Card games
  - (1) Asshole
  - (2) Kings
  - (3) Up the river, down the river
  - (4) Black or red
  - (5) High or low
- ii) Beirut (Also known as Beer Pong)
- iii) Twister
  - (1) If you're able to get a game of Twister going at a lingerie party you're basically on your way to an orgy. Good luck. The sincerest hopes and prayers are with you.
- d) Music
  - i) See **Rule #3A** for live music specifications and suggestions.
  - ii) DJs can be good at lingerie parties, too, but you have got to be on top of your jams. ****WARNING** DO NOT BE A MUSICAL ELITIST. REPEAT. DO NOT BE A MUSICAL ELITIST:** You may think dance

music sucks, but you have got to give the people what they want. Don't refuse to play something because it conflicts with your all- knowing perception of what music is, how it needs to be preserved and blah, blah fucking blah. Play good music that fits in line with all of your elitist ideas and that's fine, but also do not be afraid to put on some fucking pop bullshit and dance your ass off. You can't deny pop music is catchy. That's like declaring sour patch kids are delicious. They are. So eat them.

e) **Have a dance floor**

    i) It doesn't matter how small your dorm room is. It really doesn't. Have a raging dance party in a single dorm room. Have 10 people dancing on a single bed. Make a dance floor.

    ii) There is nothing better in this world than two women dancing in their lingerie at a lingerie party {other than more than two women dancing together in their lingerie at a lingerie party.}

OTHER THEMES:

Backlight: Tell everyone to wear white, get a shitload of highlighters, get some black-lights, turn off the rest of the lights, pump up the techno and house music and have yourself a blast.

Halloween When It's Not Halloween: Pretty self-explanatory. Costumes are the shit.

Halloween When It Is Halloween: Again, pretty obvious. Holidays exist so we can party. They're an excuse to rage. Take advantage of all the holidays.

Christmas

Mardi Gras

July 4th

Thanksgiving

President's Day

Hanukkah

New Years' Eve

New Years' Day

The Day After New Years' Day

The Day After The Day After New Year's Day

Cuanza

Festivus

Labor Day

Columbus Day

Martin Luther King Day

If someone famous dies, a celebration of [insert dead person's name here] day

Chinese New Year

Groundhog Day

Passover

Easter

Tax Day

Mother's Day

Black Friday

Day Rage: Party during the day. Make it on a Saturday and have the arrival time set at something like noon. Plan a kick-ass party, the only difference is, it's in the middle of the fucking day. People get amped up about day drinking. It's exciting. Have a few beers and look outside and see nothing but blue skies and wild times ahead. Drinking at night feels so hidden. There isn't enough light. Open those shades and get the party started, people.

Black Tie: Everyone loves getting dressed up for no reasons. Get some classy ass invitations, cheap finger foods (cheese cubes, bagel bites, what the fuck ever), cheap-ass champagne, plastic champagne glasses and go to town.

Valentine's Day: There are few things better for someone who's single than a bagin' party on Valentine's Day. It's the reason why it isn't listed in the list above of all the holidays you need to throw a party for. It was purposely left out of that list so we could discuss it here in length. What, you think Valentine's Day was forgotten? Why is it awesome to throw a party on Valentine's Day? Because it guarantees that every person who shows up is gonna be single. No single person in the history of the world ever wanted to sit around and think about how they're gonna be alone for the rest of their life. Whatever. Get some chocolate, fake flowers and celebrate all the freedoms of being single.

RULE #6(B)

A GREAT PARTY CAN CHANGE THE WORLD

Party throwing is a sacred art form. A great party can positively change the course of human history, inspire great cities to get built, and get you laid.

RULE #7

BEWARE OF PSYCHOS

RULE #7(A)

PSYCHOS COME IN ALL SIZES, SHAPES, GENDERS, COLORS, AGES AND OTHER TRAITS

RULE #7(B)

IT MIGHT TAKE YOU A WHILE BEFORE REALIZING THAT YOU KNOW, INTERACT OR EVEN ARE FRIENDS WITH A PSYCHO

He or she goes to the same school as you so they're normal, right? This might not be the case. College creates a strong sense of camaraderie, and you may very well want to trust many of your fellow students, but it's crucial to remember that it takes a while to really get to know someone, and before you start trusting Boris, Blanche, or the kid at the end of the hall most commonly referred to as "Pinky Swim-Trunks McGee" with your social security number, it's a wise choice to determine whether or not they're a psychopath.

You never know who you're going to meet in college, and even though certain people may appear just fine, it's hard to know what's boiling beneath a person until you spent a good amount of time with them. You don't have to be paranoid that everyone you run into is going to turn out to be a sociopath, but it's a solid idea to be on the lookout. Lying about important issues is a sign that someone is capable of pulling some nasty shit.

RULE #8

GO DOWNTOWN

Most women are psyched when their lover goes down on them, and even though cutalingus is a tough art form to perfect, practice makes perfect. Be sloppy and go to town.

RULE #9

READ THE SYLLABUS

It's often the simplest revelations that lead to the greatest discoveries. What do you think it was like for Albert Einstein when he realized that no piece of matter can travel faster than the speed of light? Now, that truth is common knowledge, but back before the roaring 20's when Al was sitting around twiddling his thumbs as a goddamn patent clerk conducting experiments in his head because he was a fucking genius that no one recognized until he thought his way to a bunch of the greatest discoveries of all time, he, too, perhaps, could have benefited from knowing that if you actually read the goddamn syllabus that your professor passes out at the start of every college class it's going to increase your probability of getting a solid grade by a statistic a super computer broke while trying to compute. Granted, that particular computer, the HPL75000, was built by Boris Reinhold, no doubt one of the strangest wanna-be smart people whose actually an idiot to ever walk the earth, but there was a good amount of faith in the guy.

In any event, a solid professor creates a comprehensive syllabus that outlines what's going on in the course. It's a good idea to read it and keep it handy. If you're confused about something at any point in the semester, the syllabus is a good thing to reference.

RULE #10

WATCH PORN AND TAKE NOTES

Yes, we're all aware porn is generally a superior masturbation method to relying on your own imagination, but if you'd keep your genitals in your pants for two goddamn seconds while watching porn, you'd see there's a lot to learn from the way porn starts get down. This is true for everything from positions to cutalingus methods, and if you're reading **RULE #8** and wondering what to do while you're facing off with the all mighty vagina, there isn't any shame in taking a load off one afternoon, watching some porn and taking some thorough notes on the subject.

RULE #11

LOCATE THE CLIT

If you pinpoint the clit's exact location your life's a heck of a lot easier. This is no simple task. The female anatomy is a strange and magical place comparable to the city of Atlantis in wonder, mystery and depth. On your search for where the clit is and how to fondle her, you may acquire the sensation of a scuba diver plunging to the depths of the ocean in search for something believed to be lost but you know is there and real and just as powerful as the sun or the moon. Locating a woman's clit and rubbing, licking and playing with it well leads to the following aspects of your life becoming better:

1. **Waking up in the morning:** A woman who knows you can satisfy will wake up and want to hook up. To wake from a pleasant dream and put your tongue in another more pleasant and wonderful dream is a truly great part of being alive. If a woman is nice enough to let you down there, embrace all the majesty the vagina has to offer. Try out new things, and don't be afraid to switch your speed and tenacity. Consistent rhythm with either your tongue or lips can bore, and the last thing you need is a female improperly satisfied by your mouth.

2. **Not wanting to die:** Even though life can be a somewhat pleasant experience, and the hope is you'll take part in great times while in college, there are sections and happenings that suck and make you wonder whether this whole life thing is worth it. By locating the clit and making sure a woman is pleased, the thought of death is so far out of your mind that you may even find it takes several moments after you're done going down on a girl to remember that one day you are indeed going to die, and before you do it's probably a good idea to go down on another girl or the one that you just stopped pleasuring.

RULE #12

FIGHTING MIGHT BE THE EASIEST WAY TO GET KICKED OUT OF COLLEGE

It doesn't matter how big you are, what you look like, what skin pigment you've got, where you grew up, how incredible you think you are, or anything else; the fact remains that getting in a fight either on campus or while living in a place affiliated with your college is one of the easiest and dumbest ways to get kicked the fuck out of school.

RULE #12(A)

IDIOTIC QUESTIONS START MORONIC, POINTLESS FIGHTS

Yeah, we're at the absolute pinnacle of forward progression and human evolution, but amidst all our blinding sophistication, there are millions of women and men all over this great nation parked in front of the TV watching two grown, half-naked men rock each other in the face until one's unconscious, the other is victor, and the viewer is either joy-filled or in a fit of rage. Whether it's boxing or MMA, war or Jersey Shore, hand-to-hand combat is part of the fabric of who we are as a species, but there's a time and place for all things face-slugging related. As we've been discussing and as we'll continue to research and evaluate, there are tons of times fighting is dumb, and here are some of the most idiotic questions that get people moronically fired up enough to start swinging at each other for no reason:

1.   Are you looking at me?

This is the be-all and end-all of idiotic excuses to start fighting for no reason. A drunken lunatic believes tons of moronic delusions, so it's by no stretch of the imagination that too much booze will trick some drunk bastard that you're looking at him even though you're not. Once 'are you looking at me?' is thrown out, all bets are off. You gotta put the dukes up or get the hell outta there like Ralph Macchio almost did in "The Karate Kid" before he didn't and Mr. Miyagi had to save his ass.

2.   Were you born in a different state than me?

Some take being patriotic backwards and think it's an excuse to remain loyal to your birth state and only that state, while looking at other states like they're enemy-occupied territory. The amount of bar fights that boil down to this issue is like a barbacoa burrito at Chipotle; unsettling, and that's putting it mildly.

3.   Are you rooting for a different team than me?

There's nothing wrong with healthy competition, it's what has made this nation great for over six thousand years, but rocking a man in the face because he roots for another sports team is like refusing to eat sesame chicken once you've found out it's actually pigeon. If it tasted good before you knew it was pigeon, then who cares?

4.   Did you take my seat?

For some drunk bastards, once they sit down, the seat becomes their property. There's no doubt the rules and inner-workings of public space seat claiming are intricate, but a drunken physical assault over sitting rights is a poor evaluation of priorities.

5.   Is that my beer?

No, it isn't. If it's in my hand, it's my beer, and I don't steal beer, so what are you talking about? If this were your beer, you'd be holding your beer, but because it's in my hand, it's my beer that's the end of it.

6.   Are you talking about me?

No, I wasn't talking about you. What are you, deaf? You read lips better than anybody in the tri-state area and have now decided to use your talents to decipher if I made fun of your sweater two minutes and six seconds ago when you got back from the bathroom and had toilet paper on your shoe? Screw you.

7.   What's your problem?

A derivative of "Are you looking at me?" this poor random excuse to start a fight is as irrational as they come. This question can apply to absolutely anything, and generally is used when a drunk hasn't gotten laid in about three months and is so frustrated that he hasn't yet gotten tail he's ready and willing to drop a "What's your problem?" to ensure a fight for blowing off steam purposes. Problem is, it's the wrong stream.

8.   Do I look like I'm kidding?

Generally a follow-up question to "Are you kidding me?" this zinger takes a joke that you told five minutes ago and turns it into the truth. You were joking, yes, but now that "Are you kidding me?" has been asked and you answered with "Do I look like I'm kidding?" somebody better take a swing at someone because no one's kidding now.

RULE #13

IF YOU'RE HOOKING UP AND YOU FEEL LIKE YOU'RE GONNA CUM, DON'T PANIC. GO DOWN ON HER AND REGAIN COMPOSURE

This is a classic porn-star technique. Originally pioneered in the late 1970's by a Russian gymnast named Filat that turned to the pornographic arts after falling off a tightrope that was only three feet off the ground but as Filat took the short three foot journey to the floor of his apartment, the tightrope that he'd rigged up with bungee cords across the length of his room snapped, whipped around, and the metal part of the bungee cord connected with Filat's ankle with such incredible force that it shattered it beyond repair. Even though the ankle did heal to a certain extent, the damage done to the essential sections of an ankle used for balance and such were removed. Broke, homeless and alone, Filat did the only thing an ex-Russian gymnast with a surprisingly massive penis could do; he moved to the United States, traveled to California and became known as "The Moravian," an eccentric alcoholic porn star who, while drinking, also developed hopes of one day becoming a professional opera singer. His singing was subpar.

Regardless of all this, Filat "The Moravian" Russian porn star guy realized the first day on the set that the woman he was about to have sex with was hotter than every woman he'd ever slept with combined. Less than a minute after he entered her, the size of her beautiful jugs, the sweetness of her face and the immaculate vagina that lived between her legs let Moravian know he wasn't going to last long in there without exploding all over the place. It was at this moment in a back studio somewhere in the depths of California that Moravian realized he had to do something and fast if he was going to preserve his load. After all, Moravian knew he had to get paid, and according to section 95C of the Pornographic Banging While You're on Camera regulations, a man only gets paid if he's able to hold his load long enough for the studio to get all the shots they need. So Moravian went down on Britney, and he stayed down there for a damn long time. While down there he was able to gain composure, get it together, and get right back in there swinging.

Although a champion of this newfound sexual exploit, Filat came to an unfortunate end when he was banging seven chicks at once in a suite on top of a speeding train that derailed. Filat was preceded by two bastard sons, both conceived to D-list porn stars who made their careers in voice acting porn. This is one of the world's worst creations known to man. It's where untalented, off-off-off Broadway actors go to perpetuate their dreams of one day making it big in acting. All they end up doing is talking about their sexual exploits that are minimal at best. Their experience stems mostly from attempting to obtain the sperm of producers.

But this is not about banging producers. In the late spring of 1987, Trevor Tin, a fraternity brother of the Delta Epsilon Lambda Sigma of Gamma Iota, was doing some research with a VHS of porn that he found in the depths of his fraternity's files, and realized the technique that Filat "The Moravian" was executing. Trevor began using the technique yielding superb results. Word spread about Trevor's superior techniques in the bedroom and he was able to date one of the hottest girls on campus for six months and nine days.

RULE #14

USE A CONDOM WHEN YOU HAVE SEX SO YOU DON'T GET HERPES

RULE #14(A)

THERE IS NO CURE FOR HERPES

Seriously, there's no cure for herpes. There isn't. It won't go away. You can't get rid of it. It's for life.

RULE #14(B)

GETTING LAID ONCE YOU HAVE HERPES IS HORRIFICALLY HARD

RULE #14(C)

YOU DON'T WANT TO GET HERPES

RULE #14(D)

WEAR A CONDOM WHILE HAVING SEX SO YOU DON'T GET HERPES

RULE #14(E)

THE PILL DOESN'T STOP HERPES

RULE #14(F)

HOPING YOU WON'T GET HERPES DOESN'T STOP HERPES

RULE #14(G)

PRAYING DOESN'T STOP YOU FROM GETTING HERPES

RULE#14(H)

FOR THE LOVE OF GOD YOU DON'T WANT HERPES SO JUST USE A FUCKING CONDOM

RULE#14(I)

THE DUMBASS PERSON WHO THINKS HE DOESN'T NEED A CONDOM 'CAUSE HE'S NOT GONNA GET HERPES IS THE DUMBASS PERSON WHO GETS HERPES

RULE #14(J)

DON'T HAVE UNPROTECTED SEX WITH HOMELESS PEOPLE BECAUSE YOU MIGHT GET HERPES

In all honesty, this isn't an attack on the homeless. It isn't. This country's socio-economic climate is fucked, and there are plenty of people out there without homes who are perfectly decent, but have tremendously bad, bad luck. All that's being suggested is if you do intend to jump on a man or woman living in their own filth and cardboard box at the corner of 33rd Street and 8th Avenue in Manhattan, use a condom. Even though there is nothing to indicate something like this scenario has occurred and been good, it doesn't make it out of the realm of possibility, and furthermore, illustrates how imperative it is to use protection while you're having sex, because herpes is bad, incurable, and in order to have sex with homeless people and make sure you don't get herpes, you need to use a condom.

Just use a condom so you don't get herpes.

RULE #15

CARRY A CONDOM

You've gotta be prepared for whatever the college Gods throw your way. Can you predict the future? Are you a psychic? Who knows what's gonna happen? The way to ensure best outcome is by arming yourself with the proper tools for battle.

What if you're about to get down and you don't have a condom? Check out what happened to this pour soul. He was attending a distinguished school in New York City in the spring of 2011, and he wrote this document as a cautionary tale for those who believe there's no need to carry a condom.

Back on St. Mark's Place, Hillary prefaced inviting me to lunch by saying in her calm, southern twang that she needed to speak about something tragic and math related. We're in the same calculus class. It concerned me, the word *tragic*, and it's why I agreed to meet her without hesitation.

I'm sitting in a booth at Roberto's, a little Italian place in the West Village. This menu's elaborate. Shit, look at these prices. What's in the penne vodka, enlightenment? My God. How can they charge this much for noodles? If you're gonna go to college in New York City, make sure you've either got about twenty two thousand dollars saved up or a rich Aunt who constantly sends you care packages with stuffed animals stuffed with thousand dollar bills.

Hillary walks in and closes the door quickly to keep out the cold. The young couple by the door notice Hillary's innocent, petit features. Their eyes adjust as she glides by.

The waiter who sat me, a well-built dude with a fine looking suit, begins walking towards Hillary but understands she's striding to me. The owner-ish looking guy behind the bar is a bit entranced by Hillary as she removes her coat and scarf to reveal the small, brown dress that's hugging her nicely. I guess life really isn't all that bad. I don't why I was so worried about exams in the first place.

"Sorry. I had to talk to Professor Long," Hillary says while sitting across from me at the booth.

"No problem. How do you like him? He teachers physics, right?"

"Yeah. He's a great Professor. Last class he told us all we need to howl at the moon more. It's not such a bad homework assignment."

"That's great,' I laugh. 'I've heard he's a riot."

The waiter comes over and says, "Anything to drink?"

"Just water for now, thanks," Hillary says.

"I'm sorry to jump right into this," I say, "but your inquiry concerns me. What's wrong?"

"Well, there's nothing to worry about," she says while opening her menu.

"Tragic. You said tragic, yes?"

Hillary adjusts. It makes me wonder what's going on beneath that brown dress.

"No," Hillary says while still checking out the menu.

"But, you said that. You used that word," I say.

"Oh, don't take things so literally, dear. Tragic is just a word I said because I knew it'd get you here. That's fair, yes?

"Not really," I say.

She adjusts the bust of her dress. It lightens the tension.

"Well," I say, "I'm relieved everything's fine."

"I like when you're relieved," Hillary says. She's raises her left eyebrow.

"In what way?" I ask.

"Well, I just hate to see you so stressed in class. Calculus is tough. It bothers me when you're stressed. Once relief sets in it's really a wonderful feeling, don't you think?"

"Yes, I guess," I say.

"It's warm in here, yes?"

"Yeah, it is a bit warm."

"Whenever things get warm like this I try to find something nice and moist to cool me down. It's what's best for cooling things down and releasing tension."

The waiter's standing by the table, overhears Hillary, coughs and starts choking on nothing.

"You alright?" I ask.

"Yes, sir. Sorry about that. Have you decided what you'd like to eat?"

"I still need a minute," Hillary says. The waiter nods and leaves.

"Marshall, do you mind sitting next to me?" Hillary asks. She gestures at the empty space in her booth.

"Why?"

"I want to tell you what I meant by *tragic*," she says.

I move and sit on her side of the booth. She gently rests her hand on my right thigh.

"My dorm is a block away, Marshall."

"Really?"

"Yes."

"You live in Rogers?"

'Yes."

"I've heard great things about that dorm. How do you like it?"

She moves her hand into my crotch.

"Can you comfort me there? Over this whole incident I need advice with?" she asks.

Now I'm following Hillary up the stairs. I had to give my ID to the security guard working at the front desk of the dorm. We're making our way to her room. She takes out her keys.

Hillary kisses my cheek, unlocks her door and we enter into her living room. An entire wall is lined with windows. There's a view of MacDougal Street below, and the dorm is nicely furnished. She takes off her coat and hangs it in the closet beside the kitchen.

"Sit on the couch," she says.

I obey. The painting above the television is of a woman sitting beneath a tree laughing.

"Do you have a roommate?" I ask.

"Barely. She's never here."

"That's nice."

Hillary sits next to me.

"Now we can talk," she says while leaning towards me. Her breath is beside my ear. "Is that alright?" she whispers.

"Yes," I say while kissing her cheek. I adjust my head and begin making out her full lips. She quietly moans and starts messaging the inside of my left thigh.

We're kissing deeply now, and I bring the top part of her dress down. I caress, but am careful not to pinch her too forcefully. Her slight moans encourage, and I move my tongue from her taught lips, down to her neck. She grasps the back of my head. While pulling her dress down and off, the light purple panties she's been hiding are in view. I kiss the outside of them.

"Do you have a condom?" she asks.

"Not on me, no," I say.

She stops and says, "Okay. Can you go buy some?"

I pull my pants up and move to the door.

"Yeah, I'll go get some."

"Don't get the fire and ice," she says as I exit out of her dorm and head down the stairs. "They feel really weird."

I'm out on the street searching for a deli. An elderly woman with a large bag shuffles beside me. She's talking to herself, speeds her pace, loses her footing and takes a dive onto the pavement. Shit, that didn't look good. She's on the ground. I have to help her. This isn't ideal. I crouch.

"Are you alright?" I ask.

"I don't know. Please help me. Call an ambulance."

"Alright."

"Did you see what God just did to me? Did you?"

"Not sure if that was God, lady. I'm calling the ambulance.'

"Wait here with me until it comes," she says as she grasps onto my shirt.

"I'm calling help, but I really have to be going."

The phone is ringing.

God.

Damnit.

"Yeah, Hi. Hello. I'm on MacDougal Street and an old woman just fell, we need an ambulance."

"Stay with me until it arrives, please. Will you?"

"Alright."

Instead of playing the no pants dance with a fine young lady, this bozo is left with an old woman who's fallen and can't get up. He might get some sympathy points after the whole ordeal blows over, but if he'd had a condom on his person, in his pocket when he needed it, this wouldn't be a cautionary tale of how many old ladies fall down and can't get up if you don't carry a condom, it'd be a story about love positions and happy times. While he's patiently waiting for the ambulance to arrive so this old lady can be on her merry way, there's a very upset young woman waiting in her dorm room believing a man she thought was attracted to her just bolted without saying a word.

Don't make old ladies fall over and avoid pass up golden opportunities. Carry a condom.

RULE #16

ONE TRULY GOOD WOMAN IS BETTER THAN TEN HORRIBLE WOMEN

This is a common misconception that seems to dominate much of contemporary American culture. For some reason in this country the larger the quantity you have of something is always better, but there are a shitload of things this doesn't apply to, and getting with women is definitely one of them.

What would you rather have? One smoking hot chick that's cool and you get along with, or ten ignorant bitches that you can't stand? The answer is obvious.

Now, this is not a declaration that you need to cling to the first chick that's nice to you. Dating until you find someone you really like is one of the greatest things this country has to offer. All that's being stated here is that there's always going to be the desire to get new pussy, but you have to weigh that desire against what you've got. If you're with a great woman that makes you happy, don't be so arrogant to think there are an abundance of those chicks. And if you're currently hooking up with three chicks at the same time and they're all fucking idiots with no moral compass or decent view of the world, you may realize pretty quickly the feeling in your gut that's similar to a dead animal being stuck in a well is probably caused by the fact that you don't have a good woman.

Even though the perspective so far with **RULE #30** has been from the male position, it of course applies to a woman's conquest to find a good man.

RULE #17

DON'T PISS OFF YOUR PROFESSORS

Now, what must be understood before moving forward is, as with anything, there are exceptions to every rule. That's a fact of life. There's no doubt there are dickhead professors of every race, creed, gender, appearance and so on, and this is by no means an invitation to take ridiculous bullshit from a professor without doing something about it.

Occasionally, bad people are hired by colleges and universities. It isn't unheard of. If you get into class on the first day and your professor makes some horribly racist remark about Obama, or you, or one of your classmates, it's a good indication to get the fuck out of the class and adjust your schedule. It's one of the many reasons why the add/drop period at the start of every semester exists. The add/drop period is there for you if you do want to take a class that you're enrolled in for whatever reason. It's also a good time to try to figure out if your professor is a psycho asshole. But, if you find that the professor seems pretty decent, entices you with an enlightened perspective, or seems like she's the most knowledgably person to ever study microbiology, and she hasn't said anything you deem offensive or inappropriate and decide you want to stay in the class, it's important to realize that now you're in the class, and this professor will be assigning you a grade.

Pissing off a professor that's going to assign you a grade at the end of the semester is like telling a chef at a restaurant to go fuck himself before he makes your food. After being told to fuck off, do you think the chef wants your meal to taste good? Do you think the chef might do something gross to the meal to make sure you have an unpleasant experience? If you give someone shit that's preparing your food they're gonna do something to your fucking food that'll either send you to the toilet or the emergency room. It's really not all that different with your professors, so be pleasant to them. There's no reason to be an asshole for no reason in general, and especially to someone that's going to have a pretty significant impact on your grade point average. A professor is in control of your grade, and if you don't think professors give breaks to students they like, then you're dumber than Kate Upton's left breast.

RULE #18

SIT AT THE FRONT OF THE CLASS

Put yourself in the shoes of your professor. What are you thinking when a student walks in and sits at the front of the class? Fuck, how about even if she sits *near* the front of the class? Even though this may not seem like a huge deal, to start off the semester on the right foot matters. In reality, the semesters aren't all that fucking long. They fly and are over before you know it. This is a rather sad reality of college, but nevertheless, due to the finite amount of time a professor is actually in the same room as you, things like where you sit and whether or not you seem to be paying attention matters more and more as you move forward with your college experience.

Even if you start off the first few classes by sitting in the front and then gradually move to the middle it can have a positive impact on not only your participation grade, but your overall grade in general.

RULE #19

PHYSICALLY ASSAULT THE OVERACHIEVER·

Should he or she not welcome your friendship while you're mooching off their homework, a quick and swift clock to noggin will quickly reassure them of their priorities.

RULE #19(A)

IGNORE RULE #19

The data calculations just went off the rails and we're doing everything in order to make sure things are back up and running. Although it can be a positive thing to become friends with those who study a great deal and have a natural talent for all things related to schoolwork, creating a friendship based purely on the fact that someone can help you out academically can backfire. You don't want to use people. Using people is like lying, and lying is bad, so using people is bad, too. Also, the bit about hitting said overachiever needs also to be stricken from the record completely.

RULE #20

USE THE GYM

Why?

1. **Blow off steam:** There's a lot of pressure in college. Between professors breathing down your back, GPA worries, the constant judgment from peers, and worries about life after college, it's amazing anyone makes it out alive. If you ever feel incredibly frustrated with work or issues with friends of lovers, head to the gym, get on the fucking treadmill, and let that machine help you run all that pent up anger and aggression away. The time some people spend screaming at their significant other for no reason other than aggravation with life's troubles is enormous, and much of said time could be spent getting in shape. The body needs to release all the pain that goes along with being alive. This shit isn't easy. The world is constantly in tumult, but a great way to deal with any issue thrown at you is to buck up and hit the gym.

2. **The freshman 15:** If you're worried about the freshman 15, take advantage of the facilities. Many colleges have damn good exercise equipment, and since you're paying for it, there's no reason not to jump in there.

3. **There might be a pool:** If your school has a pool, swim in the fucking pool. Who doesn't want to go swimming? Even though the open swim hours may be weird, figure that shit out, get your trunks, and hop on in. This is also an opportunity to get a group of people together and see what you all look like half naked. It's a very un-creepy way of getting just a bit more comfortable with those friends you've been thinking about pursuing.

4. **Meet new people:** The gym is a great place to meet. You automatically have something in common. A complication of ways to break the ice while at the gym are below.
    i. "That looks tough."
    ii. "Having fun?"
    iii. "Do we have a class together?"
    iv. "I've seen you here before. How's it going?"
    v. "Hey, I'm {your name here}"
    vi. "Hi, I'm {your name here}"
    vii. "How are you? I'm {your name here}"
    viii. "Hello, I'm {fake name here}"
    ix. *disregard viii
    x. *the ingrate responsible for viii is now being lead out of the building in handcuffs and will be somewhere with no light or video games for the remainder of the Twilight Zone Marathon. This is the type of shit that really gets people in trouble. Lying about your name? Why in the fuck would you do

that? This is unacceptable. Ron Peterson takes full responsibility for this and he'll pay dearly. Today we're getting KFC, and if you think he was the most excited about it, you're right, and that means he's sad now, won't get chicken, and we're all happy he won't and that's the end of it.

RULE #21

WHEN YOU SMOKE TOO MUCH POT YOU MIGHT THINK YOUR HEART STOPPED. IT DIDN'T

Many people think pot is a victimless drug, but it's not true. Sometimes you're a victim of your own paranoid, borderline insane thoughts.

Picture yourself sitting on a comfortable leather L couch in the living room of one of the more nicely furnished homes on campus, surrounded by your peers who are all excited about the party planned for later in the evening, the sun has just set, the air is cool and crisp, and there's a beautiful, picturesque view of the central quad, and all of a sudden the weed that you've been smoking hits you with tremendous force and BOOM: you're believing the unreal is true. Here you are, stoned out of your mind, screaming at your friends to check your pulse because you're certain your heart stopped. You're the victim of high quality marijuana nuggets.

As we're learning more and more everyday because of huge advancements in marijuana legalizations and discoveries, weed really isn't bad for you. Yes, it's true, that if you place marijuana nuggets in a joint with a bunch of shit you gutted out of a cigarette, roll that spliff up and smoke away, your lungs and throat and body will suffer negative ramifications, but that's pretty much only because you just mixed the soothing and wondrous marijuana plant with the poisonous dreck found in regular cigarettes.

Contaminating the glorious and all-knowing power of the marijuana plant with cigarette poison and rat shit is like taking something truly beautiful and making sure it rots down to some sort of awful bowel movement.

Regardless, the other negative element often affiliated with marijuana is the actual papers used to roll up the weed. Generally, papers aren't all that great for your lungs, and even though weed fills you with a wisdom often attributed to aiding the human race to develop language and higher level brain functions, the papers are usually filled with shit that hurts your lungs. But not to fear! Smoking weed out of a water pipe is a fine way to cut down on all the bullshit affiliated with rolling aids, such as papers or blunts, and vaporizers are another expert weed smoking device designed to enhance your high and re-vitalize your health.

But alas, what to do when you've just gotten so fucking high that you actually believe your heart stopped? Just stay calm. Even though this may seem like an incredibly difficult thing to do when you're high enough to believe your entire body is crashing down to a halt and shutting off every valve, blood circuit and living mechanism, you just have to remember the high from the weed will pass and you're going to be perfectly fine.

Take deep breaths. It may seem like the most elementary of trying-to-not-lose-your-shit-because-you're-so-high methods, but sometimes the simplest equations provide the best results.

RULE #21(A)

BE CAREFUL. THIS AIN'T YOUR DADDY'S POT

The pot that's being legally grown now is maybe a thousand to sixty eight million times more potent than whatever the schwag people were smoking fifty years ago. A good weed brownie can make you see aliens and convince you the people at the end of the green space are the CIA.

RULE #22

PROFESSORS DON'T ALWAYS KNOW EVERYTHING

Who is your professor? Do you know her? Just as there are strange, deranged and borderline insane people on the street, there's a wide range of Professors you might have. Who knows what some of them are up there talking about? Maybe it's all lies? Wouldn't that be something if your professor was spewing bullshit? Well…

RULE #23

ASK THE UPPERCLASSMEN WHICH PROFESSORS ARE THE BEST

Class doesn't have to suck. Even though there will certainly be classes you'll hate, and they'll feel like you're being tortured with a Justin Bieber song on loop and a computer virus that makes it impossible for you to click on your desired Mac icon, there are also fine ways to ensure at least some of your classes are enjoyable and fulfilling.

Finding the right professor is kind-of like trying to figure out who you want your roommate to be. You're going to be spending a lot of time with this person, and if she really wants to, she can make your life a living hell. You don't want your life to feel as though you're in the second or even third layer of hell, so take steps to make sure your professors are quality.

One solid way to do this is to ask the upperclassmen which are the best professors and why. Now, obviously you don't want to ask just any dumb shit-head who their favorite professor is and take that information as gold, but if you find someone you trust and they share similar interests, it's probably a good idea to get their advice. This is also a pretty damn good conversation starter. Whether you're at a party or at an event thrown by the school, this is a good question to spark up a conversation, and you might just learn something pretty fucking valuable, too.

Another angle is to reference certain websites that let you know what the best professors are. Some sites rate professors and you can read what other students think about classes and whether or not the professor is a piece of shit, and even though you have to take this type of online crap with a grain of salt, there's nothing wrong with getting on the internet and trying to do some research about this. Some of the sites are pretty damn informative.

RULE #24

STAY ORGANIZED

In the midst of all the debauched buffoonery taking place in college, things like times and dates can fall at the wayside pretty easily. Make sure to be on top of your shit. It's all good to have a great time and experience college for the truly fun time it can be, but unless you keep your grades at a somewhat decent level, you'll find you aren't in college anymore.

The guy or gal who wakes up after a semester of insane partying with a zero GPA finds that they're packing their bags and going the fuck back home faster than you can say keg. Not only will this be an absolutely massive waste of money, but it happens more often than you'd think. No one is immune to the low-grade getting-booted-out-of-school scenario, and a good way to make sure you'll stick around is to stay organized and be aware of important dates you have to hit for your classes.

Whether this is getting a giant calendar whiteboard to hand-write all important information for your classes on, or using a calendar program on your computer to help, the bottom line is if you want to stick around you gotta stay on top of your shit.

RULE #25

COCAINE IS STUPID

This over-priced, piece of shit drug turns the user into a complete fucking asshole. If you want to empty your entire wallet on a schedule II drug that makes you feel like God for fifteen minutes and the biggest piece of shit for the next two hours, go right the fuck ahead and pay a shit-load to some piece of shit drug-dealing asshole, but if you're gonna do it, realize the entire high is based on wanting more, and there's never, ever enough, unless you want to end up in the hospital and then in the slammer.

RULE #26

COLLEGE IS A BUSINESS

Even though every college and university puts up a front like they're a charity or a version of the Red Cross, once you sift through all the bullshit, college is a goddamn business just like any other one. You think division I athletes who don't know how to spell their first name are recruited so they can do well in the college version of a fucking spelling bee? Hell no. They're recruited for one fucking reason and that's to make the school as much goddamn money as possible. Institutions of higher education are designed, run and established to make a few administration people at the top of the totem pole as much money as a fuckhead banker or asshole stockbroker. The amount of colleges and universities in this country that are money making machines is a goddamn travesty.

So why is any of this relevant other than it'll probably piss you off? If you keep this in the back of your mind with everything you do in college it'll make your life a shitload easier. It doesn't matter if you're dealing with the RA's or trying to set up some club on campus, if you see your school for what it is and what the administration wants, you're going to have a much easier time getting away with the shit you want to get away with, and having a fucking blast while doing it.

RULE #27

THE DRINKING AGE SHOULD BE 18 BUT IT'S 21

Regardless of the fact that a person who's legally able to go fight and die in a war should have the right to drink a beer, and that's just one of thousands of arguments that render the drinking age in this country ridiculous, the drinking age technically is 21.

If you're underage drinking, a cop can fuck you over. You think a cop wants to give you a break? Some schools call the cops on students who are underage drinking in their dorm rooms. Look into if this is the way things go down at your college, and if it is, make note of it. If so, it should probably dictate what you do drinking wise.

If you aren't 21 and you're gonna drink, take the necessary precautions to make sure you don't get fined, arrested, written up, marked, tailed, cited, ticketed or whatever your school calls getting in trouble. If you do decide to get a fake ID made, realize that you're probably gonna fork over anywhere between a hundred and two hundred bucks for something that might not even work, or may get taken by a bouncer at a bar. Getting an old ID from an older sibling or cousin or friend is typical and generally more effective, but keep in mind it's possible for a fraudulent ID to be dealt with in a serious legal way. Memorize all the information on the ID that you've got, as these will be the first questions the bouncers or liquor store people ask you. Underage drinking in college is like jaywalking; technically it's illegal but everyone does and cops generally don't give a fuck. The problem is, a dick cop can do whatever he wants.

RULE #28

DON'T BE A BUM, AND DON'T LISTEN TO THE BUMS WHO TELL YOU TO BE A BUM

It doesn't matter if you're attending the worst college or the absolute best, you're going to meet, be aware of, or maybe even be friends with, good friends with, a piece-of-shit bum who doesn't do shit. Maybe he or she is the son or daughter, niece or nephew, whatever-the-fuck cousin of somebody on the admissions board, and he got into school even though he's a fucking idiot and barely passed high school. This guy could be living next to you chirping in your ear how you don't have to do any work and it'll all be fine and the professors are lenient because it's college and the worst grade given is a C, or some other cockamamie bullshit that doesn't make a lick of sense, and the danger is that you buy in and not do shit and then you're GPA is lower than this bum's IQ.

This bum can also be female. All sexes are at risk of exposure to these types of bums who do nothing and laugh about it all the way to kick out day. There's a pathetic fallacy that you can do absolutely nothing and pass your classes. It's a dumb tale as old as time that was engraved directly into the rock God emailed Jesus with the rules, regulations, triangulations and commands about what you can and/or cannot do with a woman after hours a seedy strip joint in New Jersey. There might be some confusion here. It's possible Greek mythology is being mixed up with something printed in and issue of *High Times* because weed is now basically legal and it's going to single handedly, with its almighty hands, arms and strength, pull this country out of the great recession's crest, or whatever the fuck is going wrong with all the money now, and this absolutely has something to do with the jack-off wanna-be-shoe-salesman bum guy or girl that's going to be telling you not to do any work and cut class and be a bum.

Don't be a bum, and don't listen to the bum telling you to be a bum. Sure, you can hang around with a piece-of-shit bum that's trying to convince you to not do shit and just blow an entire semester so you're GPA is so low you'll get kicked out of school and sent either back to where you came or to some other place that isn't as fantastic as college. But if you'd rather resist the temptation to be a bum and do jack shit, you can be not a bum, not waste all the fucking money that you're investing in your college education, and make sure you're motivated and thirsty for the shit your classes provide. Bums are bums.

Don't be a bum.

RULE #29

GET DRUNK AND ASK RANDOM PEOPLE FOR DIRECTIONS TO THE LIQUOR PAVILION

The best part of this is the liquor pavilion doesn't exist. It doesn't. You might think it does, and there are many activists out there determined to turn this hypothetical liquor emporium into a reality, but there's no such place as the liquor pavilion, and if it did exist, or if it one day does become an actual place, it might devalue this section slightly.

Think about the reactions you'll get when you walk up to a stranger with a straight face and ask where the liquor pavilion is. They're priceless. The tough part is staying composed when the stranger you ask actually tries to help you locate the coordinates of the liquor pavilion. Obviously, you have to stay in the joke. You can't let them know you're joking around. Even if your friends are laughing, even if the voice in your heading is screaming at you to laugh and give away that the liquor pavilion isn't real, you have to maintain that you're truly trying to get directions to the liquor pavilion.

Here are some responses you might get from people and ways to deal with them.

STRANGER #1: What's the liquor pavilion?

YOU: One of the larger and more reputable liquor pavilion's in the area.

STRANGER #2: Are you joking?

YOU: No.

STRANGER #3: Is this a joke?

YOU: No.

STRANGER #4: Can I come with you?

YOU: Yeah, sure.

STRANGER #5: Didn't I meet you at Benzo's last house party?

YOU: Yeah, that's me.

STRANGER #6: You're the third person tonight to ask me directions to the liquor pavilion. Is there something I'm not aware of?

YOU: Yeah. The liquor pavilion.

RULE #30

DORM SMOKE DETECTORS FUCKING WORK

We're in a super advanced age. Robots are about to take over the world and enslave everyone who isn't killed in the initial robot attack. If the human race is on the verge of being done away with by a superior robot computer system able to literally wipe its own ass with an iPad Air, you can bet your ass the smoke detectors installed in your dorms work.

This isn't the 1890's. Yeah, I mean, back then you could go down the street and blow someone away and get off scot-free, but now, if you smoke in the goddamn dorms and the smoke detectors are working and active then something called an alarm is going to go off, the entire building will evacuate, and you'll have to deal with the consequences.

RULE #31

DON'T PULL PRANKS AFTER 3AM

2:59 am is the cutoff. It's just the rule.

RULE #32

DON'T SMOKE CIGARETTES. THIS ISN'T THE FUCKING 1950'S. THEY'RE CANCER STICKS

The cigarette is a blemish on an already disturbed society. It's well understood we need all kinds of substances and external forces to keep us from jumping off buildings, but cigarettes have just got to stop. They're designed for kids. It's one of the first dumb things kids are able to abuse. If you're a fifteen-year-old and think you're cool because you're skipping school and smoking cigarettes, that's just fucking great for you, you little prick. Good for you. You're such a badass. You just got to middle school and now you're smoking cigarettes and doesn't that just make you the tits? No, it doesn't, and if you haven't realized how dumb it is to fork over God only knows how much green on a pack of cigarettes, you deserve to die of cancer.

Yeah, there's no doubt cigarettes look cool. Everybody knows that. They make you look like a dragon. You're just breathing fire right out of your face. And they're used in the films all the time for the same goddamn reason. The smoke looks really cool. But none of that bullshit matters.

Alcohol makes you feel incredible, and even though it's addictive and bad for you, in moderation it isn't all that bad. This is not true of cigarettes. It's not worth getting lung cancer. It just isn't. Cancer is horrible, and even though there are so many things that give people cancer, there's nothing that gives people cancer faster and more effectively than cigarettes.

RULE #33

ASK QUESTIONS

People are perpetually worried they're going to look dumb. It's a constant in the universe as real and true as that apple that fell on Isaac Newton's head, and the stain left behind when you accidently pour a coffee all over your friend's couch.

This fear of appearing stupid makes people not want to ask questions, and it's something you gotta get over the second you step on campus. If you're sitting in class and your professor is explaining the solution for a proof on your calculus exam and you think about asking a question because you're utterly lost and unaware of which way is up, but you don't, feeling as though you'll look it up later, or you'll ask one of your friends to explain it, you've already lost a great deal. Just raise your hand and ask the fucking question. You're not going to look stupid, and honestly, who fucking cares?

Even if you're in a lecture hall in front of four hundred people, and half of them for one instant hear your voice and think, 'That's a stupid question,' who the fuck cares? It doesn't matter, and the only thing asking a question is going to do is potentially get you the right answer.

RULE #34

START WITH A SOLID GPA

College gets progressively harder, which means it's highly likely your first semester freshman year will be the easiest academically. Take advantage of this. Start kicking ass immediately your first semester so you aren't playing catch up your entire college career. While all your friends are bitching and moaning by the time sophomore and junior year rolls around, whining that they have to compensate for slacking off their first few semesters and earning a 2.0 GPA and if they don't kick it into high gear their resume is gonna look like shit, you'll be sitting pretty with a 3.7 without a stress in the world. If you get a C in a class, it's a 2.0. You don't want a 2.0 GPA.

RULE #35

TWITTER IS FUCKING STUPID BUT SOMETIMES IT'S A GOOD WAY TO WASTE TIME

Follow and tweet to us at @87CollegeRules

RULE #36

DON'T SMOKE WEED IN THE DORMS UNTIL YOU KNOW HOW TO GET AWAY WITH IT. THE AMOUNT OF KIDS KICKED OUT OF COLLEGE IN THE FIRST WEEK FOR SMOKING WEED LIKE IDIOTS IS HIGH

Even though weed is about to be legal, there are still certain states that hate it, and many college administrations are ready to kick somebody out of school for smoking a joint, dooby, wopper, wambo, cramshot, behemoth, giant-fast-acting gargantuan, mammoth, mile-high plunger, dinosaur, or blunt. This isn't saying you shouldn't smoke weed in the dorms. Once you have all the necessary information, you've collected evidence, surveyed areas, conducted research and done your homework, go right ahead and puff away. But until then, realize that the RA's are on the lookout for it and you need to use the necessary precautions to avoid expulsion.

RULE #37

JUNGLE JUICE RECIPE:

1 Big Vat
1 Serving Solo Cup
1 Bottle of Everclear Vodka
1 Handle of Shitty 80 Proof Vodka
1 Bottle of Shitty 80 Proof Rum
1 Bottle of Peach Schnapps
5 Liters of Sprite
3 Cartons of OJ
2 Bottles of Sunny Delight
8 Liters of Mountain Dew Code Red
5 Liters of Mountain Dew
1 Bottle of Purple Drink
And as much Sour Patch Kids candy as humanly possible

RULE #38

WATCH YOUR DRINKS

It doesn't matter what sex you are, it's a good idea to always be aware of where your drink is and who handles it. Even though you may want to trust everyone you meet in college, you never know who is a creep, asshole, douchebag, fuck-head or dick. If you show up to a party and someone hands you a drink, it might be fine, but the fact that a person had control of the drink before it was handed to you, makes it slightly suspect.

Bottom line, be cautious with how you get your drinks and what you do with them. It's not necessary to be the most paranoid person on the planet about this shit, and generally it's alright to trust people if your instinct directs you that way, but you have to be aware that there are fucking asshole college students out there who roofie people. It's definitely a shitty aspect, and even though it may seem like no one does it or it's impossible that someone is that much of a fuck-face, it's a sad reality that's still an issue in colleges and universities all across the United States.

Don't leave your drink unattended. For example, if you're gonna step out of the party, don't leave your drink behind and then grab it once you re-enter. If that means just throwing it out, that's fine. Who cares? Even if it's a beer or some other drink in a container that doesn't seem like it's easy to roofie, it's definitely something to keep in mind.

Also, if someone gives you shit about these issues, and is trying to convince you with vehemence that you have nothing to worry about concerning roofies or anything like that, mark them as a creep and tell them to shut the fuck up. Even if it means you get thrown out of a party, it doesn't fucking matter. Anyone who doesn't respect someone's wishes to be safe and cautious about this shit doesn't have their head on straight.

It's often the people that you'd never expect that turn out to be the creepers. You know when news reporters interview the neighbors of a serial killer and they all say they never saw it coming? It's kind of like that. Now, there's no doubt that when you get on campus there's an energy and mayhem that makes people want to go a bit wild, and that's fine, but you always want to be aware of where the threats are, and as long as you're cautious about who's handling your drink and how it's attended, it can help you avoid something potentially horrible happening.

RULE #39

REJECTION IS BETTER THAN REGRET

A magnificent American named William Yessirman once said, "You can't win if you don't play." Good God was he correct, and even though this expert advice applies to a great many things ranging from attempting to fit a keg through a dorm window, to trying to spark a massive party with little more than a thirty pack of beer and a dream, it especially applies to trying to find a mate, or partner, or love, or whatever you want to call the person you're actively trying to hang out with and engage in sexual activity.

Nobody ever spoke to a member of the opposite sex, went on a date, got laid, or had a threesome, without actually going up to someone and initiating conversation. Take Martin Timothy Henry III; Marty to most of his friends and family who constantly made *Back to the Future* jokes whenever he was around to harp on his name being Marty, like Marty McFly, so you didn't spend too much time with Martin Timothy Henry III before someone yelled, "Next Saturday night, we're sending you back to the future!"

Marty enrolled in college in 1985, and on October 3rd of that year, he was standing in the main living room of a house party. His school was located just outside Pennsylvania in a New Jersey town many still adore because it seems like it's part of Pennsylvania. In the midst of the mass confusion erupting all around Marty because of the beer pong games going on in the right corner of the living room being played on some of the longest tables ever constructed, Marty wondered what he was doing with his life. He had a beer in hand, and he was enjoying himself at the party, but there was something missing in his life. Unsure of exactly what that thing was, while standing there in an utter daze, Maria Gambino walked by and a light the size of a blimp went off in Marty's mind. Maria wasn't just looking good, she had an Italian allure to her that rivaled some of the finest Italian cuisine those small hole-in-the-wall places have that you discover while walking down a cobblestone street in Rome. Even though Maria wasn't the most beautiful woman on the face of the planet, she knew what she had, what she didn't, and how to use her keen sense of style to accentuate what worked for her. She looked great.

Little did Marty know, Maria had just gone through a pretty devastating breakup and wanted to make out with a girl and a guy at the same time in the worst way. Marty got the eyes from Maria, approached her and asked if she wanted a drink. The rest is history. On October 4th, 1985, somewhere in New Jersey that's close enough to Pennsylvania to feel like it's in Pennsylvania, therefore making it a rather pleasant place to walk around, Martin Timothy Henry

III made sweet, sweet love with Maria Gambino and her friend Sarah Ross.

Make the move. Make it.

Maria was the two hundred and fifty sixth female Martin Timothy ever hit on.

RULE #40

HITTING ON WOMEN IS A NUMBERS GAME

It's just like sales; the more leads the more women. Despite all the leaps and bounds American women have made concerning the workforce and every other section of life, it still remains that a man is expected to walk up to a woman and initiate conversation. It's just the way it is, and considering the founding fathers were abiding by the same standards, rules and codes of ethics, when it comes to the man approaching the female, it's clear it'll last probably until we're all blown up by either some awful war or an asteroid slamming into the earth.

If you walk up to a woman and she's not into it, don't sweat it. There are more than 300 million people in this goddamn country, and that means just about half or more are members of the opposite sex. If one girl in a bar isn't into what you're serving up, it isn't the end of the world. Far from it. All it takes is realizing that she has her priorities out of whack for overlooking your greatness, and move on to the next potential woman of your dreams.

Who knows what some females are going through? You can approach a girl in a bar who's been in a relationship for two years and is probably going to marry the guy while you're none the wiser. Why beat yourself up if she isn't into you? There are few examples of a single night's hitting-on ripping apart a meaningful relationship.

RULE #41

PICK YOUR ROOMMATE BATTLES

Unless you really get a roommate from hell and all the papers need to be filed in order to change roommates, you're going to be stuck with your roommate for at least a semester or two, so pick your battles with all things living arrangement related.

While living with your roommate or roommates, problems are going to arise. Below is a list of just a few, represented as questions.

1. Did you have a party in my room and not clean up anything?
2. Why the fuck didn't you ask me to leave before you started having sex?
3. I'm pretty sure whoever you brought home last night stole three of my Gatorades and a brownie.
4. Is this yours? Why is it on my side of the room?
5. Did you leave that on my bed? Why was it there in the first place?
6. Where are my Miller Lights?
7. Where's my peanut butter?
8. What happened to the peanuts I had right here?
9. Where's my alarm clock that goes off 16 times before 8 am?

10. Who put this in the trash?
11. Have you ever done the dishes?
12. Can we talk about how loud your music has been?
13. It's your turn to clean the toilet.
14. How long is your friend staying on the couch?
15. What do you mean, you didn't know she was my sister?
16. Why is it my turn to take out the trash?

And these are only the beginning. The thing to remember is, you want to pick your battles. If you're able to let something that bothers go, let it go, especially if it isn't all that important. For the issues that really bug you, just talk to your roommate about it in a civil way. Don't present it to them as if you're attacking, but bring it to their attention to create a living environment that everyone can enjoy. Stay calm, and reinforce that you're just trying to make the living arrangement work. It's also a good idea to avoid bringing up issues when either you or your roommate is drunk. The alcohol is only going to create a greater potential for one or both of you to fly off the handle and go bezerk.

RULE #42

COFFEE AND WHISKEY

Booze and coffee are the two things that cure hangovers. Combine them and say, goodbye hangover. The only danger here is it could allow to drink all day and have an even worse hangover the day after that. Prepare yourself if you're going to embark on a coffee and whiskey journey into drunk town, for the caffeine will give you fuel, and the booze, a false sense of everything, including confidence and all the rest.

RULE #42(A)

COFFEE, WHISKEY AND BAILEYS

This is an even better combination. The Baileys acts like a creamer.

WARNING: If you drink an entire (750ml) bottle of Baileys, or even a significant portion of one, you're guaranteed to puke.

RULE #42(B)

8oz. COFFEE, 2oz. WHISKEY, 3oz. BAILEYS, 2oz. COCONUT WATER, AND FILL WITH SOY MILK

This is the best hangover cure. This recipe was given to Moses by God himself, but due a series of other demands, God made sure this secret has been kept a secret in order to discourage alcoholism. It's even rumored the recipe had something to do with the 11th commandment, but this has never truly been confirmed. God's fear is if such a remarkable and effective hangover cure is released, it will cause too many alcoholics for the planet to handle, and could start a chain reaction that unravels at least three other dimensions other than our own.

RULE #43

NICKNAMES ARE GREAT. CREATE THEM FOR YOUR FRIENDS

EXAMPLES:

Lorne Michaels
Fun Bags
RIP
Blown
Rummage
The Dietitian
Shrunk
TittyFuck
The Blind Arsonist
Metal Monster George
The Real One
The Awful Insomniac
Trick Leg Lenny
The Riot Generator
Pink Nosed Rambo
The Rack
The Prison System
Boris The Hummer
Big Bean Tori
Helium

RULE #44

BECOME FRIENDS WITH MEMBERS OF THE OPPOSITE SEX BECAUSE IF YOU DON'T BANG THEM YOU CAN BANG ONE OF THEIR FRIENDS

Randall Sinks was sitting in his house in a mildly comfortable chair at school in 1999. It was almost midnight on a Thursday and he was trying to figure out what he was going to do. Can't waste the night, he thought. I can't waste this night.

All of a sudden, as if some higher power was listening to Randall Sinks' cries of woe and desire to have fun and not waste the night sitting around doing jack shit, Sinks got a call from his friend Carla. After some pleasantries and jibber-jabber, Carla asked, "What are you doing?"

He'd made friends with Carla freshman year, and even though he'd thought about it many times, Sinks never tried to hook up with her. This showed her that he was able to become friends with a girl just to be friends, and not want a BJ or anything else related to getting jiggy, or down, or getting himself all up in her lady parts. And on this night of nights when Carla called, she was calling because she had a friend who wanted to engage in sexual activity with a nice guy.

Jenny Manning needed a referral. She had needs, and wanted to engage is some hand stuff or even some mouth stuff with a guy, but she didn't just want to go to some random party and play Russian roulette with whether or not she was actually going to meet a halfway decent guy. She needed a referral, so she called Carla. This is one of the beautiful things of having friends. Referrals. Some people are not good at making friends and spend their entire lives locked away in their rooms wondering why despise the human race so much, and there's nothing wrong with this type of person. Some people don't like making friends, but if you have any aptitude for friend-making, there's a wide array of reasons why it's positive, and something to be valued.

Jenny Manning and Randall Sinks hit it off right away. They both liked baseball and wondering what jokes their Professors would deem most offensive. They even discovered that they both had uncles that were raised in Bristol, Rhode Island.

You think Randall Sinks was pissed while Jenny Manning was being incredibly nice to him physically while he was also being really nice to Jenny Manning's private anatomy? No. Jenny Manning wanted something and she spoke with Carla and Carla threw the referral Randall Sink's way. Even though Sinks still had to prove that he had the goods once he met Jenny Manning, because Jenny trusted that Carla wouldn't steer her wrong, she had the confidence to go with her gut and think fondly of Randall all the more.

A solid Thursday.

RULE #45

IF YOU WANT TO GET AWAY WITH SHIT, KNOW HOW TO TREAT AUTHORITY FIGURES

1) **Befriend authority figures.** Sounds a bit crazy, right? Just the whole idea of seeking out good graces with people who are able to get you in serious trouble starts out as a wild idea, but upon examination, it makes total sense. You're absolutely more likely to get away with shit if you're friends with authority figures. Take cops for example. If you're friends with Officer Hersey, what do you think are the chances Officer Hersey is going to arrest you? You'll probably have to do something pretty fucked up for Officer Hersey to take out his handcuffs, tie you up with them and toss you in the back of his cop car, so unless you're planning on killing somebody, by befriending Officer Hersey, you've now set yourself up with a license to get away with a ton of illegal shit. What happens if you're speeding and Officer Hersey pulls you over? Nothing. And this is just the beginning. A friend who has the power to get you off the hook and give you a free pass is a powerful friend, and it's where this entire idea of befriending authority figures is derived from.

a) Now, in college, resident assistants, or the **RA**, are a common form of authority figure that are able to fuck you over. Generally, resident assistants are the police officers of either the dorms or on-campus housing. It's their job to make sure none of the rules are broken, and due to the fact that the drinking age is still 21 and not 18 for reasons that are completely moronic and insane, there's one rule right there you may want to break so you can chill out and drink a beer. In all seriousness, how is it that the drinking age is 21? A woman can go into a voting booth at 18 years-old, help decide who's going to be the leader of the free world, but once she gets back home and wants to have a glass of wine, it's against the law? What the fuck is wrong with this country? Anyway, it's a damn good idea to establish a pleasant relationships with RAs that are in your immediate radius. This doesn't mean you have to suck up to them or become their best friend if you don't want to, it's just a reality about college that it's a good thing to be pleasant to the RAs that could very easily fuck you over for a thousand different violations ranging from simple partying to going completely out of control.

b) Any **Dean** of anything is someone you want on your side. There are tons of ways you're potentially going to run into a Dean over the course of your college career. Maybe you join a club? And at one of the meetings the Dean of Campus Life makes an announcement that she's going to be working with whatever club you're a part of, and if you have any questions to feel free to ask her at the end of the meeting. It's not the worst idea in the fucking world to go up to Dean Campus Life, introduce yourself like a decent human being, and establish some kind of relationship with her. This way, if she sees you again, she'll remember how well-mannered you are and it might just come in handy down the road.

i) WAYS TO MAKE A GOOD IMPRESSION ON AUTHORITY FIGURES

(1) Be polite. "Please" and "thank you" sometimes. Dean Jonathan Wilber of a college we can't locate the actual name for once fired his own cousin from the position of Dean of Environmental Affairs because the cousin didn't say "thank you" after being shown a cupcake with the school's crest painted on it in pink icing.

(2) Don't swear.

(3) If you feel like you're going to get upset about something, just smile.

(4) Listen to what they say. You can't respond intelligently if you don't listen.

(5) Take your time.

(6) Don't say "like."

(7) Don't say "um."

(8) If you need to take a pause instead of saying "like" or "um" just take a pause. There's no need to rush. A strong, dignified pause is a great moment for you. Don't blow it by nervously sputtering a preposition.

(9) If you're dealing with an authority figure over a non-violent issue, repeat, "We aren't hurting anyone," over and over again.

RULE #46

IF A GIRL GIVES EYES IT INCREASES THE CHANCE OF INTERCOURSE BY 67%

It's the year 2000, and this girl's name is Wendy. She's standing just outside an administration building properly named "The Back" because it sits at the back of campus and the guy working the front desk usually has his back to you when you walk in because he doesn't much care about what people think or why he's there.

On this overcast Wednesday, Wendy is alone and cute and has decided if she meets someone decent-looking and charming, there's a high probability that she'll engage in at least some type of sexual activity. It's a quick thought, this recognition that she wants to fool around with someone worthy. She hasn't done anything like this in a while, and even though this is out of her character, she wants to and needs to clear her mind. Her classes are incredibly difficult and demanding this semester, and it's really turned her world around, having to realize that classes are this hard and in order for her to get good grades and a solid GPA she's going to have to work harder than she's expected. Wendy is aware of the kind of energy finals is going to require; she has to clear her mind and recharge her batteries somehow.

She's standing in front of this administration building called "The Back," and even though there are guys walking by that are making her wonder if she'd like to kiss one of them and then see where things go, they aren't noticing that she's looking their way.

She even spots Jared Rush, and he's really in a rush, but does see that Wendy gives him eyes, smiles, and is waiting for him to rush over and talk to her. Because he isn't aware of the fact that if a girl gives your eyes and a nice smile it means there's a higher probability that she's into you, he rushes by and heads towards his dorm to do something meaningless.

Wendy is left there, and she eventually walks over to the cafeteria to try and deal with her frustration some other way. She does enjoy a good cup of yogurt every once in a while.

RULE #47

THE PROPER TERM FOR DUMB SHIT YOU DO WHEN YOU'RE FUCKED UP BECAUSE YOU THINK IT'LL BE FUNNY IS "MISTAKE"

Tony and Steve both recently started their sophomore year of college, but they're at Steve's house in Arkansas because it's spring break. They're gonna hop on a flight to Vegas the next day and spend the week gambling, going out, drinking too much and trying to explore all that Las Vegas, Nevada has to offer. They also recently discovered Steve's dad's liquor cabinet.

Three-quarters of the way through a bottle Tony settles on the idea to play drunk catch inside the house but Tony doesn't have a ball. He grabs a vase on top of the mantle. Steve runs and Tony fires off the vase like he's playing Madden, and the thing hits Steve right in the hands, but it's no use. Steve bumbles it. The vase smashes. Dust goes everywhere.

"Fuck!" yells Tony.

Steve is laughing and doesn't care.

"I'm totally fucked," says Tony.

"Why? It's just a vase."

"That was my grandmother, dude. Fuck. You gotta help me most of her in this trash bag."

"Why did you play catch with her?"

RULE #48

GUYS GUIDELINES FOR PROPER TINDER USE

1) Always swipe right. #NumbersGame
   a) Tired of swiping? Download an autoliker. Autolike girls in the hundreds, even thousands, with just one click.
2) Turn off push notifications. This may seem counter intuitive, but forces you to respond randomly. This ensures you don't come off desperate. You are only available when things are convenient.
3) Get to the point quickly. Don't send more than five messages without asking the other party out for drinks.
4) Never ask questions. Always make statements.
   a) Bad Example: Would you like to get a drink?
   b) Better Example: Let's grab a drink. Free tomorrow? You're getting laid with that line, my friend.

RULE #49

DON'T RAT OUT YOUR FRIENDS. DON'T NAME NAMES

Even though resident assistants, security officers and many other authority figures working in higher education hide behind a collegiate facade, make no mistake, if a college is investigating an issue, they're just a few steps away from actually being cops. In many cases this can be a good thing. If someone steals your laptop right out of your dorm-room when you left it unlocked by accident, you're going to be thrilled that you can write out an official report through the college and send security offers out to try to recover your lost merchandise. This is true of a great number of issues ranging from physical assault to date-rape and everything else you can think of.

There is another side to this, though, and in the same way that cops wrongfully accuse people of all kinds of crimes, the same is true on college campuses. Some colleges even create online databases and interfaces that allow students to anonymously post if they've seen someone commit a crime. So, for example, if the guy across the hall has it out for you and sees you sneaking beer into the dorm, he can theoretically go onto to one of these sites and post what you're doing, with the intention of getting you caught and punished. This also opens up the door for people to post all kinds of stupid shit that has nothing to do with anything; the only intent being to get you in trouble.

In any kind of investigation, authority figures are going to want names, and whether you've actually done something wrong or you've been wrongfully accused of something, it isn't a wise idea to throw your friends under the bus. Sometimes they'll ask who you hang out with only to try and get the names of other students they can try to accuse and get in trouble and pin something on. Sometimes naming either the people you know or friends of yours is unavoidable, but by in large try to be as vague as possible when it comes to the people you want to protect.

RULE #50

DON'T GET ADDICTED TO ADDERALL

Prescription pills are all over college campuses, and because Adderall is not only legal but prescribed, it's rampant. Some people legitimately need medication, and that's fine, but if you're cramming for a test or need to write a paper in three hours, Adderall may seem appetizing.

You gotta remember that Adderall is essentially speed. It's highly addictive and prolonged use sometimes causes suicidal thoughts. That's when the voice in your head starts thinking it's a good idea to go launching yourself off a high rise without a parachute strapped to your back or some guy that rips the chord so you land safely on the ground. The dangerous thing about getting addicted to something is it's really fucking fun to get addicted to something. The giant problem is once you're addicted, you're a prisoner and a slave to the substance. Experimentation is fun and fine, but an addiction will put your life in the shitter, and being in the shitter blows.

RULE #51

START MEDITATING

If you're already aware of how great meditation is, then good for you. If you're unaware, get on it. There're lots of ways to meditate, but the crux of it is to sit down, get comfortable, relax, close your eyes, and focus on your breathing for about twenty minutes. Maybe throw on some classical music? It's a positive way to recharge the batteries, and if you think it's dumb because you've got limitless knowledge and you aren't willing to explore new areas of thought for two and a half seconds, then go fuck yourself.

Meditation is a pleasant stage between being awake and asleep when you can let thoughts pass by peacefully without reacting to them. Dealing with all the craziness going on in the world is a harrowing task. After meditating you're going to feel more pleasant about yourself, your surroundings, and in general you'll just feel refreshed. Is it as drastic as taking a hit of acid and listening to an entire run Phish did at MSG during New Year's 2011? No. But instead of forcing your brain cells to have a heart attack, you'll give them a nice break and they'll appreciate it.

It relieves tension and stress, and allows you to look at the world in a generally more peaceful way. Instead of getting angry about something and throwing your desk through your dorm window, just meditate.

RULE #52

NEVER HANG ON TOO LONG. THE SECOND YOU SENSE A SIGNIFICANT OTHER NEEDS SPACE, GIVE HER SPACE

{The following is a transcription of a speech Edward Trident delivered in a dimly lit restaurant in a bunker in the Hudson Valley in the late 1800's [the exact date is lost]. It's theorized that the actual headless horseman was present for the talk, and even though he had his head at the time, it wasn't too long after the speech that the headless horseman did lose his head, and even though it has nothing to do with the speech that's transcribed below, it is a note attached to another note that's attached to the transcription}.

Edward Trident: Ladies and gentlemen, brothers and sisters, friends, adventurers, explorers and all the rest, I want to sincerely thank you for coming. There aren't too many days where we can meet here. Times are tumultuous, yes, and the world turns in ways that scare, excite and send better men than I into a rage, but what's necessary for us to know, is that at the center of all of it, whether we want to admit it or not, is coitus. Coitus, you may be thinking? Yes, coitus. Coitus. Coitus, everyone. Beneath all of it is coitus. It's the fundamental truth that drives everything forward, and without it, not only would life cease to exist, but it'd be much, much cheaper.

The reason why I've called for this emergency meeting to discuss coitus and its influence on mechanics and modern day reasons for staying alive, is not so much to give a talk and have a discussion on its significance, but to discuss the complex art of sparking true curiosity in a significant other. The only way we're going to make sure people aren't going to off themselves by jumping off bridges and eating cod until they can't breathe, which, rest in peace farmer Jim; you were a man far too great to force yourself to suffocate on cod, and the reasons you did so are mysterious, but, in a roundabout way, I think talks like this will prevent such things from occurring in the future, and shape a better tomorrow we can all look forward to.

Anyway, let's get right down to the nitty gritty of this. Right down to the brass tax. When you're wooing a woman, or a man, for that matter, it's important to respect their space. No one likes to be smothered, suffocated, bombarded, attacked, or berated, and even if you and your significant other or potential significant other are hitting it off, if smothering occurs, and the glorious feeling of freedom is lost even the slightest bit, it can really do damage. Don't be afraid to give your lover space, and don't take offense to this, either, if they need some time alone or time to reflect on themselves. This desire to have space doesn't necessarily reflect poorly on you.

Some examples: if your lover seems down, and she clarifies that it has nothing to do with you, and other sad things are going on in the world that are making things difficult, offer support, but by no means become angered if your attempts at cheering her up fail, or if it seems like a good idea to leave. Again, it's as important to know when you and your lover need to be together as it is to know when the two of you need to be apart. Also, let's say your lover isn't all that interested in an invitation you extend because she's feeling a bit under the weather; an inexperienced person will believe the lover is lying and try to guilt said person into attending the event, but an experienced, confident person, aware that their lover is probably just feeling a bit under the weather, will not push, but instead give the love the space she needs.

RULE #53

USE THE OWL PURDUE WEBSITE

Worried about MLA formatting issues? No problem. Google: Owl Purdue MLA Formatting.

RULE #54

COORDINATE STUDY GROUPS

Yes, it'll beneficial to your grade. It'll help. It will. Studying with your peers, people also trying to learn, will increase your chances of studying and learning. It's also an awesome way to get to know people, make friends, and decide who you're going to be talking to for the rest of life. It's true, you're going to probably make life-long friends while you're in college, and one of these bonds could very well form while you're reading Marx's *The Communist Manifesto*. Books this incomprehensible need to be spoken about with other people. There's no other way you won't go totally insane while reading it and other books like it. A book like that can re-configure the ground that you stand on, and you start having bad dreams.

RULE #55

EAT BREAKFAST

If you scoff at this rule you're gonna be in a world of hurt. You can't run solely on coffee and a shower. It's not wise. You're gonna find yourself furious and not know why, and it's just because you didn't provide your body with fuel upon waking. It doesn't have to be sausage pancakes and six eggs or anything, but a piece of fruit or a bowl of cereal in the morning can do more for your happiness than you'd think.

RULE #56

USE THE BINARY SYSTEM

The 1-10 scale is a dumb pissing match. "Oh, she's a 8 cause she's got better tits than your chick," or "He's a 6 cause he's short and ugly," or any other of the moronic things people say to put themselves above other people. It's all a crock of shit. Get with the times. Binary, people.

1 = YES
0 = NO

Just fucking decide. Do you want to be with that person? Yes or no? Figure it out and leave it at that. There are more important things going on in the world.

RULE #57

GET LAID AS MUCH AS POSSIBLE.
THERE ARE PLENTY OF DAYS IN A WEEK

There are seven days in the week.

RULE #58

RUM IS GOOD WITH PINEAPPLE JUICE

RULE #58(A)

DRINKING RUM AND PINEAPPLE JUICE, STATISTICALLY SPEAKING, MAY LEAD TO AN INCREASED POSSIBILITY OF HAVING SEX

RULE #58(B)

TEQUILA AND PINEAPPLE JUICE, STATISTICALLY SPEAKING, ALSO INCREASES THE CHANCE YOU'LL ENGAGE IN SEXUAL ACTIVITY

RULE #59

YOU DON'T WANT TO PICK UP THE DRUNKEST CHICK AT THE PARTY

RULE #59(A)

RULE #59 IS ONE OF THE BIGGEST ROOKIE MISTAKES IN THE BOOK

RULE #60

TO MEET SOMEONE, ALL YOU GOTTA DO IS BE CONFIDENT

RULE #60(A)

YOU CAN LOOK LIKE A FUCKING SHOE AND AS LONG AS YOU'RE CONFIDENT AS HELL YOU CAN PICK UP PEOPLE WAY OUT OF YOUR LEAGUE

RULE #61

YOU WANT TO PICK UP THE HOTTEST CHICK AT THE PARTY, NOT THE DRUNKEST

RULE #61(A)

IF THE HOTTEST CHICK AT THE PARTY IS ALSO THE DRUNKEST, OMIT RULE #61

RULE #62

TREAT GOOD LOVERS WELL

For whatever reason, whether if it's the fault of movies or music or TV or MTV or YouTube or whatever the fuck is rotting people's brains on a consistent basis, but there's shit flying around the culture that tells people it's cool to treat your lover or lovers like complete shit. It's not fucking true. It isn't. The people who let you have sex with them are awesome, and when you find a good lover that's fine and good, you wanna treat them well.

RULE #63

GET A GOOD PAIR OF HEADPHONES

For many, college is not a place where there's a lot of privacy. A quality pair of headphones lets you check out. It's a good option to have if you're ever feeling like you need to get the fuck away from everyone but you have to stay in the dorm.

RULE #64

DON'T DRINK AND DRIVE

Getting drunk is one thing, but if you get drunk and get behind the wheel of a two-ton death machine, you've just drastically upped the chances something completely fucked up is going to happen. It isn't that easy to kill somebody by accident when you're drinking beer and laughing your ass off at a party, but it's pretty damn easy to accidently kill someone when you're driving drunk. The thing you wanna look out for are the people who get some sick high from driving drunk. For whatever reason, some people just get their kicks from driving drunk. They think it's cool. Maybe they get some high from the adrenaline? It's fucking ridiculous. There are plenty of other ways to feel alive and dangerous than potentially killing yourself by driving drunk on the highway.

RULE #65

A BROWN BAG LIQUOR DRINK COVER WORKS SOMETIMES, BUT NOT WHEN YOU ACT LIKE AN ASSHOLE

The law says if you're in public drinking a beer that's in a brown bag you can't get in trouble, right? Nah. It's bullshit. But that's not to say you can't try. If you're acting like a decent human being a cop might even let this slide, but if you're running around yelling, "WHO WANTS TO TOUCH IT?" there isn't a shot in hell you're getting out of a ticket.

RULE #66

HATEORADE IS HALF GATORADE HALF VODKA

Want to walk around campus with a beverage in hand without making it obvious? Put some vodka in your Gatorade bottle and you're good to go.

RULE #67

TIME TRAVEL IS POSSIBLE. ALL YOU NEED IS A FIFTH

It's believed time travel isn't possible. It is. You ever drink so much that you're standing in your living room one second and the next you're at a bar across town but it's actually two hours later and you've got no fucking idea what happened for that two hour period of time? That's time traveling. You wanna avoid it. People do terribly stupid things when they're in a blackout, and during the time you're time traveling, you're blacked out. In order to time travel you have to drink enough for the front section of your brain to shut off. Once this front part is off and no longer functioning, then it means the back section of your brain is in control, and the back part is basically equivalent to a gorilla's. Learn to fucking pace yourself. There's no reason to race and see who can black out the fastest. Try getting laid when you're blacked out and see how that works out for ya. The coolest person in the room is not the one that can drink the most.

RULE #68

BE ON YOUR BEST BEHAVIOR AROUND COPS. THEY CAN DO WHATEVER THE FUCK THEY WANT

Seriously, cops can do anything. It's your word against theirs. How do you think that's gonna go?

RULE #68(A)

THE COPS CAN THROW YOU IN JAIL AND JAIL IS BAD

RULE #68(B)

JAIL IS FUCKING HORRIBLE

RULE #68(C)

NOT GOING TO JAIL SHOULD BE AT THE VERY TOP OF YOUR PRIORITY LIST

RULE #68(D)

IT'S ALL FUN AND GAMES UNTIL SOMEONE GETS ARRESTED AND GOES TO JAIL

RULE 68(E)

IF YOU HAVEN'T BEEN ARRESTED AND YOU HAVEN'T GONE TO JAIL, YOU WANT TO KEEP IT THAT WAY

RULE 68(F)

ADJUST YOUR BEHAVIOR TO MAKE SURE YOU WON'T FUCKING GO TO JAIL

RULE #69

MAKE A BUDGET

Money sucks but it's a necessary evil. Even though there's the strategy of just emptying your entire checking account at the bodega's ATM, spending without discretion and hoping for the best, this tactic generally results in the money running out and a hobolo Joe existence setting in.

Just map out how much money you have, how much you'll make over the course of the semester, and figure out how much you can spend per week. If it helps to make a daily budget, then crunch the numbers that way. Remember that the entire reason college exists is so you can get a job that will pay you money, so there's nothing wrong with saving money now so you'll have a little bit of coin when you graduate.

You're gonna have to put a security deposit down on the hypothetical apartment you'll get after school, right? You think that shit just pops out of nowhere? Not everybody has a fucking trust fund. If you're around kids like that at school, trust fund pricks, and they're blowing all their parent's money like it's nothing, and you're not in that position, don't feel pressured to blow all your hard earned dough just because you're surrounded by spoiled jackasses. Someone who's just getting money handed to them by their parents isn't aware how fucking hard it is to save money.

It doesn't take a rocket scientist to realize that college students who become pill heads are probably getting all the fucking cash to fund their drug problem from their parents. Don't fall into this crowd, and don't blow all your money on bullshit.

The prick who wants to unload his entire paycheck at the bar isn't aware of how things really work. Yeah, it's great to go out to the bar and have a good night, but if you're handing over hundreds of dollars on booze that you can get at the liquor store for less than twenty bucks, something has done awry.

RULE #70

START A BAND

There's nothing people in college like doing more than gettin' drunk and going to see some live music, and if you're the one they're going to see, you're already a step ahead of the game. People dig musicians.

It's just a fact of life. If you're able to create music it instantly makes you more attractive to the opposite sex, and if you've got those gifts and you're just sitting around your room, playing for yourself, you need to get the fuck up and get on stage somewhere. Anywhere. Who cares? Get a band together. Ask around. Someone has got to know someone that plays bass or guitar or another instrument that you don't play, so get to jamming, baby.

RULE #71

DON'T FEAR PEOPLE WHO ARE DIFFERENT·

Best case scenario, college is a time when you're going to meet, get to know, become friends with, date, love and be involved with people that are very different than you. Don't fall into the stupid fucking trap of disliking others purely based on the fact that they're different than you are or what you know. This narrow-minded thinking is only going to fuck you in the end.

RULE #72

THE MORE GAY MEN ARE AROUND THE EASIER IT IS FOR STRAIGHT MEN TO GET LAID

It's a simple numbers game.

RULE #73

TOO MANY KEYSTONES MIGHT MAKE YOU SHIT YOUR PANTS

Then there's the time Bernard Hubert drank so many Keystone Lights he shit his pants. He had about fifty nicknames after that: poops, the big BM, smelly McGee, John, Lou, The Diarrhea Ninja, Bobby the Blower of Chunks Out His Ass, Dumping All Over The Place Without A Toilet Nearby Timmy; we were ruthless. Too many Keystones.

"You're drinking too many of those fucking things!" we yelled. We were screaming it all night, all over the house. That house was great. Billy Horace moved into the place his sophomore year, but when he graduated and we were juniors we took it over. Great fucking house, but way too many Keystones. Bernie just didn't listen. Us telling him to stop made it worse. I regret yelling at him to slow down.

"Lay off the stones," I was saying. I remember. He'd just look at me and say something like, "It's a free country, Mickey. And I'm freer than a convict who just got let outta the slammer and hasn't gotten laid in a year. I'm free as a beast. A wild beast. A lion."

If I'd kept my mouth shut he probably woulda taken it easy. The egging on was what did him in. He took it as a challenge. I'd say "don't" and he'd want to do it more just to fuck with me. He stayed up all night drinking. Didn't sleep. Not one wink. I crashed at like two in the morning, but he just kept raging all night. I heard he was ranting and raving to a bunch of freshman that the Titanic was an inside job. I'd heard him go off on that rant before. He'd use the living room like an executive board room. He'd say things like, "There was somebody on that fucking boat that wanted it to go down, I'm fucking telling you."

I can only imagine what that rant was like after a thousand Keystones and not sleeping. He'd harp on the fact the boat went down because of an iceberg, and say shit like, "Are you fucking kidding me? There isn't a shot in hell that fucking boat sunk by the hands of a block of ice. Water is water, yeah? And ice is water, so how the fuck does Uncle Sam expect me to believe a block of hard water took down the almighty Titanic? Huh? It was an unsinkable machine, that's what the papers said. It was an inside job, I'm telling you. Men in suits, with guns and political agendas wanted that boat at the bottom of the fucking ocean, and true to form, with their old-time bowties with top hats, they made sure the Titanic shot down to the bottom of the ocean, and stayed there. Inside job all the way, that Titanic. She was. Coulda been the same motherfuckers who faked the moon landing. I wouldn't even be surprised."

Man was he nuts, and the next morning, when we were having bacon egg and cheese sandwiches in the gazebo next to the quad, you could see it in his face, the discomfort. I can't even remember who was in that gazebo other than Bernie and me. Must have been Ritchie and Kenny. They were always around. If something fucked up was happening, Ritchie and Kenny were just there; they'd just appear, as if they were somehow connected to the winds of disaster that float around trying to find the right group of fuckin' idiots to latch onto. And in those days, we certainly were a pack of fuckin' idiots.

So, yeah, there we were, a few of us in the gazebo the morning after Bernie just kept drinking and drinking Keystones, and who knows what we were talking about, but I know we were all eating bacon egg and cheeses, and I'm certain Bernie was drinking another Keystone Light. I asked him how many he'd drank and he decided to answer me by saying he was the man, and I responded by saying that didn't answer my question, and I remember him saying something like he was the fucking man, and then we kind of started yelling at each other.

It was a beautiful day out. One of those days you hope and pray for in the middle of winter. And while Bernie was drinking this Keystone and eating the bacon egg and cheese sandwich and yelling at me, there was a moment when something came over him, and I saw his face change, and there were wild sounds coming out of his body. It was as if all forces within him unsettled, and Bernie's face went from a look of friendly argumentation to horrified uncertainty.

He looked right at me and said, "I don't feel good anymore. I have to get somewhere." I asked him, "What do you mean? Where do you want to go?"

And that's when a groan came out of his stomach that I've only ever heard similar on The Discovery Channel. Not only did we all hear this in the gazebo, and looked around at each other in utter amazement that such a sound came out of a human being, and that the human being was indeed Bernie, the next noise that broke the tense feeling had more force.

Louise Timber, a short, cute blonde who just happened to be walking by the gazebo heard it. She looked towards us, expecting for there to be an animal to account for the incredible groan, but there was no animal; just Bernie.

What happened next I'm going to explain in an unorthodox way. It's too disgusting to explain what actually happened. Instead, I'll replace all of the grotesque elements with positive things, so hopefully you'll understand what Bernie did, but you won't have to go through the horrid reality of him shitting his pants.

Editing out all the grotesque elements, what happened next, was Bernie stood up. We all leaned back. The sounds ringing out were like an orchestra. It was as if an entire symphony was inside Bernard, and even though all instruments were playing loud and insanely, there was little to no harmony, and the intensity kept rising. Bernard's pants started to fill up, and it almost looked like the bottom half of him was becoming the stay puffed marshmallow man. That's the way I'll describe it, with marshmallows, to try to mask the retched truth of what happened, but show you the way Bernie was able to shit his pants like nobody in the entirety of human history.

It was around this time we were asking things like "Bernie, what the fuck?" and "Jesus Christ, Bernie, what the fuck is going on?" but Bernie was in a trance. He claims his soul left his body at this point, and even though his pants were filling up like a bag of cotton candy when the guy at the circus puts the bag right into the cotton candy machine, he was staring blankly and serenely off into the distance.

The noises got louder and louder, and the smell that began to loft was comparable to an entire factory of cupcakes, except on the complete opposite side of the spectrum. If there was anything that it didn't smell like, it didn't smell like gigantic cakes with aroma so pungent and good it makes you want them for your birthday. It was the exact opposite of that smell.

The smell was so thick it almost made Hillary Marsh fall over because was walking by the gazebo when all of this took place. She immediately started to gag, and in order for me to explain what happened next, I need to switch this mode of pleasant explanation with peaches and cream, and get real for a second. The smell was so unbearable that Hillary, who was 20 feet away, projectile vomited all over the walkway.

By this time we had all jumped out of the gazebo out of fear of vomiting ourselves or worse, and Emma took off running towards the dorm and didn't look back. Everyone ran away, and tried to get as far away from Bernie as possible. But I stayed reasonably close to him, to make sure he was still alive, and even though the smells and sounds coming out were apocalypse-ish, the moment of explosion was remarkable. His pants ripped entirely open, and everything went flying out and around like a bomb. His pants couldn't take the force. They exploded, and it's a miracle Bernie wasn't killed.

Later, when Bernie woke up in the hospital, the doctor let him know that not only had he experienced one of the most powerful and horrific bowel movements of all time, but if he ever had another Keystone Light, there was a distinct possibility his entire body would combust.

So, Bernie doesn't really drink anymore. I mean, he'll have a beer every once in a while when we get together to reminisce, but that incident scared him straight, and even though I vow to make him drink a Keystone Light before he dies, if he does drink one, he may die immediately after from a poop explosion release so bad it makes an elephant's unpleasantness look fine.

RULE #74

CHOOSE YOUR MAJOR AND MINOR WISELY

If you already have a solid idea of what you're going to major in, good for you. The first few classes that focus on your intended major will be telling of whether or not you're gonna stick with that major, or minor, or to change it up and pick another path.

If you're unsure of your major and minor, it's probably a good idea to have a conversation or two with your advisor about what you're gonna do with your life, and if he or she doesn't help you in any way, maybe ask if you can switch advisors. You're paying enough fucking money; you sure as hell want to get the types of answers you're looking for.

It's also a good thing to keep in mind that, yeah, you want to go into a profession that you're gonna love, but you also want to be good at what you're gonna do for the rest of your life.

Sometimes it's a solid idea to go into a profession that you may not be absolutely in love with, but you're really great at it. You gotta make money somehow in this fucked up world, and if that means doing other people's taxes for a living, so be it.

There are a great number of jobs out there that aren't all that romantic sounding, but they pay really fucking well, and ultimately that's important. You go to college to increase your chances of not only getting a job, but a decent paying one, too. You're not gonna win the lottery. It's just not gonna happen. Sorry. It's like a billion to one shot, and even though it sucks sometimes to think practically, it's better you do that than let the world kick the fuck out of you.

If you haven't already realized, this world is harsh as fuck, and if you think you're so far away from the homeless dude on the street, you're a lot closer than you'd think. Play to your strengths, and pick a major that you genuinely want to study.

If you're unable to somewhat passionately commit many hours of time and energy into studying, it's gonna make your major and/or minor brutal. Deciding on a major and/or minor is about finding a happy medium of an area you genuinely enjoy and find interesting, and picking a craft that you're good at.

RULE #75

IF YOU'RE PLEDGING A FRATERNITY OR SORORITY, AND THE BROTHERS (OR SISTERS) HAZE YOU BY MAKING YOU DO ANY FUCKED UP SHIT THAT YOU DON'T AGREE WITH, GET THE FUCK OUT OF THAT ROOM

RULER#75(B)

TELL THEM ALL TO GO FUCK THEMSELVES

RULE#75(C)

FUCK THAT SHIT

RULE#75(D)

THIS IS AMERICA, NOT COMMUNIST CHINA

RULE #75(E)

WHEN HAVE YOU EVER VOLUNTARILY LET PEOPLE TREAT YOU LIKE COMPLETE SHIT? DON'T START THIS IN COLLEGE, AND DON'T LET A FRATERNITY OR SORORITY MAKE YOU THINK YOU HAVE TO BECOME A BITCH FOR A SEMESTER IN ORDER TO HAVE A BLAST IN COLLEGE

RULE#75(F)

FUCK FRATERNITY AND SORORITY HAZING. IT'S BULLSHIT

RULE #76

BEFORE BRINGING UP THE IDEA OF PLAYING STRIP POKER, MAKE SURE AT LEAST ONE CHICK IS REALLY INTO THE IDEA

RULE #76(A)

THE BEST WAY TO ORCHESTRATE A THREESOME WITH TWO CHICKS IS TO HAVE ONE CHICK WHO'S REALLY INTO IT. SHE'LL CONVINCE THE OTHER CHICK THAT IT'S A GOOD IDEA

RULE #77

TRY STAND-UP COMEDY

Chris Rock worked at McDonald's and did stand up for years before he got noticed. Louis C.K. bombed the first time he got on stage. It takes thousands of hours to become good at something, and for some, stand-up comedy is a craft that's worth practicing every day.

There are comedy clubs and open-mics all across the country. Getting up on stage to do some comedy can best fuckin' thing in the world if you're the type that's gonna enjoy it, so why not give it a shot? You've seen stand-up at a comedy club or on the internet and thought, "I might be able to do that." You have. So jot down a few jokes and get on the fuck on stage.

RULE #78

WRITE A STAND-UP COMEDY ROUTINE

The lights are dim and it smells like buckets of beer are being poured onto the ground so it will freeze and people will slip and fall so others laugh.

We're at comedy night in Boston. This coffee house where they're holding this event isn't anything to get excited about there's a stage and plenty of seats.

A stand-up is on stage. Her name is Loraine Barns. She's wearing a peach colored dress and high heels. Her hair is brown, and she looks a little bit like Aubrey Plaza. It isn't her, though. Damn. That'd be sick if it were Aubrey Plaza. Whatever. Let's see if this Aubrey Plaza look-a-like is funny.

Loraine is holding the mic stand. We're waiting for the next joke, and so is the rest of the audience in here. She brings the mic closer and says, "Man, my father's nuts. He's a piece of work. The guy's a naysayer. A skeptic. He's the type of guy that could have known Jesus Christ, seen the guy do all the miracles, and he'd still be skeptical. Still wouldn't be convinced Jesus was the son of God. I can see it now, ya know? My father, two thousand years ago at the scene of the crucifixion, talking to Jacob, or something."

He'd be saying something like, *Jesus Christ, though, he really thought highly of himself. One of the more conceited guys I've met. Confidence? Please. A confident mohel snips correctly. This guy had enough chutzpah to*

*cause blindness. Yes, of course this is rough, but my cousin
Eli got it upside down for jokingly claiming divinity. He
was just drunk, ask anybody. Honestly, a simple chuckle.
You know, ironically enough it was at one of his "I'm the
messiah" parties. After a few too many glasses of wine and
a bad joke, Eli got dragged away like a scapegoat. Between
you and me, I saw him, Jesus, I saw him walk on water.
He even did a little dance, too. Was a pretty good mover.
Light on his feet, I'll give him that, but the whole thing
wasn't that impressive. Especially after schlepping all the
way to his place. It'd be a nice little thing to be able to do,
sure, but come on, it doesn't make one all knowing. Yes,
OK. But did he ever go swimming? Could he? Yes, able to.
Was he able? That's legitimate. Well, I walk on the ground
but diving into it hurts. Was it just the soles of his feet?
He's just buoyant. Exceptionally buoyant. Yes, I agree. If he
could fly it would be a different story. And yes, the wine was
pleasant, but I don't think it entangles him with majesty.
I know. I never missed them. I'm not denying his ability
to host a great party. Yes, the music, everything, fun and
good, you know that, and damn good wine, delicious, but
being able to urinate fermented grapes doesn't make you the
messiah. I've said it before and I'll say it again. Please, don't
get me started on the birth. If it's true, the implications are
just plain strange. Did she even agree? You hear what I'm
saying? Celestial being or not he still needs consent.* But
that's my father, ya know? Always naysaying. An
eternal skeptic.'

Loraine sits down on the stool that's on stage. Then
she says, "Well, you have all been such a great audience,

I have to confide in you. I gotta get something off my chest. I actually know how to travel through time. I'm a time traveler. I know. I know, crazy, right? My younger brother showed me how to do it. The kid's in college and he figured out how to travel through time. Not a bad undergraduate education, if you ask me. But, yeah, that's what I've been doing lately. Zipping around, traveling through time. And I know what you're thinking. Especially after the last joke. Jesus. What's he like? And you know what, he's actually a really fucking great guy. Really and truly. Not all that tall, but really a sensational guy. It took me a while to find him and when I finally did I said, 'Hey Jesus, I've been looking for you. I've heard a lot about ya."

And you know what he said to me? He said, "Yeah, word travels fast when you're the son of God." Anyway, so I told him straight out, I said, "I want to see some of the miracles." I told him I'd heard a lot about these miracles and I wanted to see some of them with my own eyes. So, he rounded up some of his buddies and took us all to a small lake. And I can honestly say he went right out and walked across it. Walked right across the fucking water. It was amazing! And then, while he was walking on the fucking late, he turned the water he was walking on into wine. It was fantastic. Everyone swam in it, bathed in it, was drinking it while swimming in it and getting drunk. Meanwhile, Jesus was walking on top of this lake he'd just magically fermented into wine, dipping his cup in. We were like, "Jesus, come on in the water, the wine, whatever the fuck you just did to this lake, come on in," and he was like, "Nah, I think I'll just keep walking on it, I'm good right here." But, yeah, I've been traveling all over the fucking place now that I can travel through time. It's alright aside from the re-entry burn. It's not easy to travel through time, let me tell you. Sometimes I fuck up the landing. But, it's alright. Alright, you've all been a great audience, have a great night.'

Loraine leaves the stage. The audience claps.

RULE #79

THE GRATEFUL DEAD AND PHISH USE SUBLIMINAL MESSAGES IN THEIR LYRICS TO TELL FANS TO LEAVE THEIR LIVES BEHIND AND GO ON TOUR WITH THEM

Since the moment Jerry Garcia picked up a guitar, there were stoned, drugged-up lunatics surrounding him and following him everywhere he went. Seeing live music is one of the best things in the world, but there is nothing quite like the obsessed jam band person. It's a fine thing to be obsessed with, but several scientists have discovered subliminal messages coded in every Grateful Dead and Phish song that convinces the listener to drop everything and follow the band everywhere. This is also true of several other jam bands, but their technology to integrate subliminal messages into their songs isn't anywhere near as strong as the Grateful Dead, and the only band that gives the Dead a run for their money is Phish. Just something to be aware of.

RULE #80

JUST BUY A KEG. IT'S WORTH IT

Unless you're at a school with incredibly strict keg rules, just get a fucking keg. It'll save money and beer tastes about fifty times better out of it.

RULE #81

EMBRACE SPONTANEITY

Spontaneity is inherently exciting. If somebody runs into your room and asks if you want to go see some woman give a lecture about whether or not free will actually exists, just fucking go. College is about opening your eyes and mind to new experiences, and once you learn you're way too young to know about all the awesome shit that's out in the world the better. Remember when you were two years old and learned that walking was awesome? That's what you're in college to do; learn how to walk. You think you know exactly how to walk, right? You don't. You don't know the first fucking thing about walking. Get out there and learn.

RULE #82

THERE'S A BIG DIFFERENCE BETWEEN QUALITY ADVICE AND COMPLETE BULLSHIT

Some people don't know jack shit and claim they know everything. These types are everywhere. It's usually the person who claims they know nothing that's got the most valuable information.

RULE #83

MAKE A BEIRUT (BEER PONG) BRACKET

Take the March Madness bracket and re-design it for a Beirut (Beer Pong) competition. It's these types of throw-downs that will decide who's the best and who fucking sucks.

Make a whole day of it. Make it a big production. Tell people that's it's gonna happen way in advance so everyone can chose partners, make team names and start talking shit. The more shit talk the better. For many of you, this is as close as you're gonna get to actually making it to the final four of the dance.

Start drafting up the rules. There can be no dispute over what the rules are. All bases have to be covered before the competition starts. People get killed over Beirut (Beer Pong) rule disputes. You don't want anyone losing their life because Buck McSimmons bounced and won the game and your house doesn't allow bouncing. Write up the rules and paste them on the wall so everybody knows what the deal is. Make sure to reiterate to everyone that the rules are important, non-negotiable, and any breaking of the rules will result in forfeit. Again, this is a precautionary measure so Suzy Louise doesn't win a round of the sweet sixteen with a lean that's so horrendous it was like her entire body was on top of the fucking table.

Name the event, too. Call it "Beer March Madness Death Drink Beer Festival" or something. Get a buzz going around campus about it. Let teams from all circles join in.

WARNING Make sure there is an equal ratio of guys and girls enrolled in the competition. It's a rookie mistake to only have one team of girls. This will ensure the entire fucking thing is a sausage-fest. If you're having trouble convincing girls that they should either join a team or make one to enter into the competition, say that the winner is gonna get a prize. Free beer or something. Whatever it takes. Just think of something that people will want when they win an all-day drinking competition. Maybe a bottle of tequila? Keep it classy.

RULE #84

ALWAYS NAME YOUR BEER PONG TEAM. THE FUNNIER THE BETTER

EXAMPLES:

The Screaming Yetis
The Broke Revolutionaries
The Hookers With A Heart of Gold
The Wandering Lone Gunmen
Bigfoot's Friends
The Wasted Youths
The Fall Down Blasted Drunks
The Train Wreck Brigade
The Standing Up Threesome Exchange
More Peach Schnapps Sallys
The Fuck Good Beers
The Borrowed Book-Men
The Unsinkable Titanics
The Wild Traffic Makers

RULE #85

ONCE YOU'RE IN A PARTY, NO MATTER
HOW BIG, YOU'RE IN. IT DOESN'T MATTER
IF TAYLOR SWIFT IS THERE. NOW ACT LIKE
EVERYONE ELSE IS A DICK IF THEY GIVE YOU
SHIT. YOU'RE IN AND YOU'RE SUPPOSED TO BE

Enough said.

RULE #86

GO ABROAD

Studying abroad is without a doubt one of the best and most fulfilling things you can do during an undergraduate education. Traveling and seeing new places opens your eyes, mind and essence to an entirely new set of possibilities. Not sure what you're going to do with your life? Let the incredible inspiration that'll wash over you once you get aboard tell you what your life if going to be like. Any expectation you have for what it could be like to live in Paris, or Rome, or anywhere else, will be shattered by the experience you'll have while studying abroad.

Anywhere in central Europe is a good bet. Once you're over there, the flights to neighboring countries are cheap as hell, and for the most part, as long as you stay in central Europe, you're not gonna end up anywhere where they'll arrest you for no reason and kick the shit out of you in a public forum as a means of punishment.

Regardless, if you do go abroad, you want to be as cautious around law enforcement as you are when you're in the United States. You do not want to get thrown into a jail is some fucking country where you aren't even a citizen. This needs to be repeated: do not get fucking arrested when you're in another country. Getting arrested, thrown in jail, going to court and all the rest of that shit is crazy and bad enough when you're in America; imagine doing it in a place where you can't speak the fucking language.

As long as you're careful, studying abroad is the absolute shit.

RULE #87

DON'T GET SENT TO THE HOSPITAL

If you're really sick or something bad happens, of course you should go to the hospital, but this rule exists so you don't do anything dumb to get sent to the hospital. Like drink 57 beers in a night, get sent to the emergency room and they kick you out of school for it. Don't do that.

ALSO FROM
NEW CHAPTER PRESS

**The Lennon Prophecy: A New
Examination of the Death Clues
of
The Beatles**
by Joseph Niezgoda

Offering a new interpretation of
the hidden messages and symbols
that have ornamented Beatles
mythology for years, this examination of the Beatles'
recordings and album artwork theorizes that John
Lennon's murder was eerily foretold. Following a
fascinating and unique trail of sorcery, mysticism,
numerology, backwards masking, anagrams, and
literary and theological writings, the book posits
that John Lennon sold his soul in order to achieve
international fame and fortune and subsequently paid
the ultimate price for his success.

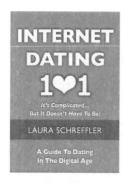

Internet Dating 101: It's Complicated... But It Doesn't Have To Be:
The Digital Age Guide to Navigating Your Relationship Through Social Media and Online Dating Sites
by Laura Schreffler

An all-encompassing guide for those wanting to use social media to look for love in the digital age, Internet Dating 101: It's Complicated But It Doesn't Have to Be! is a humorous yet helpful book that navigates the ins and outs of Facebook, Twitter, online dating sites, e-mail, Foursquare, and more. Filled with testimonials from men and women, this relationship reference also includes information on what should and shouldn't be posted on Facebook, appropriate times to tweet photos, the best and worst dating websites, and situations in which it's best to send an e-mail, pick up the phone, or simply chat in person. Arming people with the tools necessary to attract the mate they really want, this guide helps readers find out what their love interests are really like based on what they are—or aren't—saying, posting, tweeting, or e-mailing.

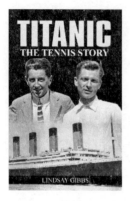

"Titanic: The Tennis Story"
by Lindsay Gibbs

A stirring and remarkable story, this novel tells the tale of the intertwined life of Dick Williams and Karl Behr who survived the sinking of the Titanic and went on to have Hall of Fame tennis careers. Two years before they faced each other in the quarterfinals of the U.S. Nationals – the modern-day U.S. Open - the two men boarded the infamous ship as strangers. Dick, shy and gangly, was moving to America to pursue a tennis career and attend Harvard. Karl, a dashing tennis veteran, was chasing after Helen, the love of his life. The two men remarkably survived the sinking of the great vessel and met aboard the rescue ship Carpathia. But as they reached the shores of the United States, both men did all they could to distance themselves from the disaster. An emotional and touching work, this novel brings one of the most extraordinary sports stories to life in literary form. This real-life account – with an ending seemingly plucked out of a Hollywood screenplay - weaves the themes of love, tragedy, history, sport and perseverance.

FROM THE AUTHORS

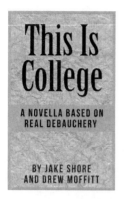

This Is College: A Novella Based On True-Life Debauchery (Kindle Ebook)
by Jake Shore, Drew Moffitt

A hilarious tale of college debauchery with a positive moral undercurrent. Dan Turner makes mistakes in college so readers don't have to. A fast paced, present tense whirlwind through New York City and Higher Education.